D1626645

Please renew/return this item by the last date shown.

So that your telephone call is charged at local rate, please call the numbers as set out below:

	From Area codes 01923 or 0208:	From the rest of Herts:
Renewals:	01923 471373	01438 737373
Enquiries:	01923 471333	01438 737333
Minicom:	01923 471599	01438 737599

L32b

HOW TO RESTORE

Classic Car
Engines

OSPREY

RESTORATION

GUIDE 8

HOW TO RESTORE
Classic Car Engines

Roy Berry

HERTFORDSHIRE
COUNTY LIBRARY
629·25
2050420

Published in 1985 by Osprey Publishing Limited
12–14 Long Acre, London WC2E 9LP
Member company of the George Philip Group

Sole distributors for the USA

Osceola, Wisconsin 54020, USA

© Copyright Osprey Publishing Limited and Roy Berry 1985

This book is copyrighted under the Berne Convention. All rights
reserved. Apart from any fair dealing for the purpose of private study,
research, criticism or review, as permitted under the Copyright Act,
1956, no part of this publication may be reproduced, stored in a
retrieval system, or transmitted in any form or by any means,
electronic, electrical, chemical, mechanical, optical, photocopying,
recording, or otherwise, without permission. All enquiries should be
addressed to the publisher

British Library Cataloguing in Publication Data

Berry, Roy
    How to restore classic car engines.—(Osprey restoration guide; 8)
    1. Automobiles—Maintenance and repair
    I. Title
    629.2′5   TL210

ISBN 0–85045–624–x

Editor Tim Parker

Filmset and printed in England by
BAS Printers Limited, Over Wallop, Hampshire

CONTENTS

Introduction

These are books on car restoration and much of the series is about refurbishing—improving the appearance of the vehicle. Certainly old car restorers care about the vision of the finished car. That vision is not, however, just about appearance. A journalist once said, 'Your enthusiast is concerned with: what it looks like, what it feels like and *what it goes like*'. 'What it looks like' goes without saying, 'what it feels like' is to do with the tactile satisfaction of trim and upholstery, of instrumentation and finished wood or of 'period metal finishes'. Both are covered in other books in this series.

'What it goes like' is the engine's province. Much of the car's personality depends on that engine. One can think of instances. 'What it goes like' is not just about 0–60 in x seconds or y miles per gallon, it can be, just as much, about 'trickling' along country lanes in a high gear with the engine pulling smoothly and quietly. It can be about the satisfaction that comes from 'meaty' torque that keeps the car in command of an increasing gradient.

I'd add 'what it sounds like'. Enthusiasts derive a great deal of pleasure from the sound of their engines, be it the crackle of the exhaust under acceleration—and sometimes its resonance on the over-run—or, the quiet idle indicative of correct carburation and suggestive of good quality engineering and disciplined maintenance.

You could just go out and buy an engine job, but clearly you've thought about doing it yourself and I suggest that the incentive to do this isn't just financial, or a mistrust of the 'professionals'. Working on an engine can prove satisfying. You'll be critical initially along the lines, 'Why on earth did the designer put that there?', but the enthusiast made of the right stuff will increasingly be drawn into an analysis of the engine from the point of everyday common sense, sound engineering, and perhaps into the intellectual pleasure of the technical design elegance. Certainly, at the fundamental physical level, there is a pleasure from handling well-made parts and from feeling fitted parts working well together.

In this book I've tried to offer something on the practical plane to enthusiasts from near the beginning stage to the person who has done several engine restorations (women can be good at it too!) Several people in this latter group find making the 'is it worn out?' descisions difficult, leading to unduly expensive restorations on one hand, or unsatisfactory ones on the other. Some advice is offered on getting equipped to work on your engine effectively. I have not, however, set out to make this chapter a comprehensive guide.

The meat of this book is a guide to the methods that can be generally applied.

From time to time you'll come up against practical difficulties. A chapter on 'nasties' details how some of these may be overcome. Finally, there's a chapter dealing with engine temperature control, or cooling system.

Finally, I would like to thank the following for their considerable help: Debbie and Alma Marrow, Ian Berry (Sun-

The donor. A 1971 P5B Rover

Above **The vision. A similar Rover V8. Resplendent and very 'torquey' in a Morgan Plus 8**

beam engine), Jack and Steve Branson (Rover engine), Howard Payne (Jaguar engine), Barry Hodges and Guy Scott. I mustn't forget the car restoration students with whom I work and especially Penny Paterson who took and produced the photographs, drew diagrams, helped with typing and generally facilitated completion of the book.

Roy Berry

Left **The challenge. Even the cleaning of this Rover V8 seemed a daunting prospect**

Chapter 1 | Getting set up

It will be obvious that a certain amount of preparation is necessary before undertaking the overhaul and exterior refurbishment of the engine of an older car. The need for suitable tools, a strong bench, and a clean, well lit, dry place to work is readily apparent. Another requirement, not so obvious is the right mental attitude in your approach to the task.

Engine restoration can be frustrating, annoying, and demanding yet enjoyable and ultimately, very rewarding. A colleague says of a mutual friend, that if he hits a snag, say a seized rocker adjusting screw, he will clean it, measure it, blow on it with an air line, hit it with a rubber hammer and then walk away, defeated. Now this man is over cautious; his way you get nothing done, but it is even more stupid to 'press on' abusing things when damage is clearly being done. In this situation it is a wise person who

Spanners: top to bottom

Open-ended spanner—metric sizes. Suitable for use on Continental and late British cars.

Combination spanner. AF sizes. Suitable for use on American vehicles and those of British origin from the mid-fifties to the late seventies.

Ring spanner. 'Whitworth' sizes suitable for British vehicles built prior to about 1954

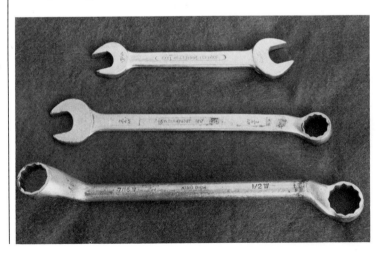

The case for $\frac{3}{8}$ in. drive sockets. This $\frac{1}{2}$ in. AF socket with the $\frac{1}{2}$ in. square drive cannot reach this fuel pump bolt on a Rover V8 engine. A $\frac{1}{2}$ in. AF socket with $\frac{3}{8}$ in. square drive did so easily

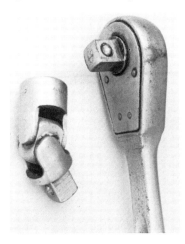

These socket set items shouldn't be used when nuts or bolts are very tight. The ratchet may give way and high torques should always be applied in a straight line, eliminating the need for the universal joint

can decide what is most expendable. What is needed is a blend of determination and discretion together with a clearly formed image of the standards *you* will settle for.

Within a generally optimistic view of the job, you will also need to take a cynical, pessimistic and critical perspective of each individual part. Be careful of trying to discover how well it has lasted, all that is OK for 'pub chat', but between yourself and your engine, be *very* critical. Try not to concern yourself too much with time. Be fussy about cleanliness during wear assessment and rebuilding. Have a good look at the workshop manual, if one is available, and try to memorize the constructional details and procedures for repair for the engine.

Think about tools and equipment. Taking the latter first, there are going to be times when a small crane is invaluable. It's plain stupid to risk injury manhandling any engine, even when it's out of the car, without some sort of lifting gear. I am lucky in that I can usually borrow a small crane. If you aren't so fortunate, then resort to the local tool hire firm.

A small oxy-acetylene welding plant used mainly, for body repair, has proved useful for a number of jobs around the engine, from loosening rusted nuts to cutting an engine out of a 'donor' in a scrapyard. Another luxury is an air compressor. A blow-gun operated from this source is very useful for clearing and checking oilways, but I do not regard either the welding gear or the compressed air equipment essential.

The hand tools that are going to be most used are spanners and here you must be certain that you use the correct size and type. If your engine is pre-1950 and of English origin, then Whitworth spanners will be needed. Unified bolts and nuts, needing spanners marked 'AF', denoting the distance 'across-the-flats' of the bolt heads, were employed from 1950 or thereabouts until the late seventies. The spanners for Unified nuts and bolts are also suitable for American National Coarse and National Fine items, i.e. for pre-war 'Yank' cars.

Some English engines, made in the fifties, pose a problem because they were built with Unified threads, but the cars into which they were fitted had earlier origins and

The home mechanic, after some
experience, may find himself
making up his own special tools,
like this valve spring compressor
for an Alfa Romeo

were built with threads to the Whitworth standard. On
these vehicles both 'Whit' and 'AF' spanners are needed,
so care has to be taken over their selection and to ensure
that bolts and nuts cannot be mismatched.

Metric threads are used on Continental cars and metric
spanners are needed for their repair. These spanners, like
those for Unified bolts, are marked according to the distance across-the-flats of the bolt head (or nut) but in this
case, the letters AF are not used.

I find that combination spanners, having one ring and
one open end, are more useful and nicer to use than the
traditional open ended spanners. The latter are not, in any
case, suitable for continued heavy duty work, since this
will cause the jaws to stretch.

Undeniably, for some work you will need to use sockets;
for undoing and tightening cylinder head nuts and those
on bearing caps and such. Here it is better and more
economic to put together a set of sockets as the need arises,
rather than to buy a big boxed set. I think that for a lot
of engine work and indeed, general work around the car,
$\frac{3}{8}$ in. drive items are preferable to the larger $\frac{1}{2}$ in. variety.
As well as being lighter, an important consideration, they
are easier to 'wangle' into inaccessible places. Some $\frac{1}{2}$ in.
pieces will be needed and you may have to buy a big $\frac{3}{4}$ in.

A *good quality* torque wrench is essential for work on aluminium engines and for some purposes on others. This type gives a signal by sight, sound and feel when the required torque is reached

drive socket, plus a ½ in. adaptor, for the odd big nut that you might encounter. Buy good quality tools!

Most socket sets include a ratchet handle. Be careful where you use one of these. The ratcheting arrangements are often not 'up to' continued heavy duty work. You don't need much imagination to visualize what might happen if a ratchet 'gave' while you were exerting a really strong pull on it. Universal joints too, are best avoided if a nut or bolt is really tight. On some the cross pins are too weak to be continually subjected to high loads.

MORAL: Use the tee bar or the sway bar to deal with the really tight ones!

A torque wrench is necessary for most engine work, it is absolutely indispensable on engines with a high aluminium content. Be wary of cheap torque wrenches. My preference is for the type that 'breaks' with an audible click when the torque setting is reached. The torque wrench should have a good long handle so that you can tighten the bolt steadily to the recommended torque without any snatching. If you find the cost of a torque wrench, daunting then hire one from a local tool hire store.

What you won't be able to hire, I guess, is a micrometer, since these are precision instruments but when it comes to wear assessment you can't beat measuring the parts.

Precision measuring instruments as used by professionals:

a External micrometer (Jaguar crankshaft)

b Internal micrometer (Jaguar cylinder block)

c Comparator. (MGA cylinder block). The instrument is rocked to and fro, the smallest reading being the correct one. The Comparator, as its name implies, merely shows variations from a standard.

Only you can decide whether it's worth investing in one of these in view of the infrequency of its use. It might be wiser to entrust the measuring to someone else but be on your guard if he has a vested interest!

Though you might consider the cost of an internal micrometer justifiable, I imagine few amateur mechanics will own, or be prepared to buy, a comparator guage, the best instrument for cylinder bore measurement. Again, you might be advised to get someone else to do it for you. There are some ways round the problem, however, which I'll deal with later.

Engine parts will need to be cleaned. The use of petrol for cleaning is very dangerous, using thinners even more so—to say nothing of the expense. Paraffin is cheaper as well as being a good bit less flammable! Keep your cleaning solvent cans capped except when filling or pouring from them. It is a good idea to wash a big batch of parts in one go and then clear up so that an open tray of flammable liquid is not left vulnerable to accidental ignition.

Finally, look after your body, it's the only one you'll have. Get yourself a good cotton boiler suit (more fire resistant than nylon), a stout pair of shoes or boots—ideally some with protected toes, some goggles—clear ones, then rub some barrier cream into your hands and you'll be ready to begin.

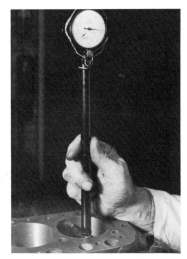

Chapter 2 | How to restore engines— in a general way

This chapter deals with engine removal, dismantling and the difficult business of deciding which parts are worn out. The reader should try to absorb the gist of this and chapter 3 before embarking on any practical work. After this specific bits may be picked out for guidance as required.

Removing the engine

If your car has a rear engine or if it has a front engine and front wheel drive, then it is going to be difficult to generalize much about engine removal. It is safe to say, in every case, that the vehicle, if lifted, should be safely supported on axle stands, that any wheels remaining on the ground should be chocked, that suitable lifting gear be used and that the first job is to isolate the battery by removal of the earth lead from its battery terminal.

Supposing that your car has a conventional front engine layout then it is generally possible to remove the engine and gearbox as a unit, or to remove the engine only leaving the gearbox in place. There are pros and cons of both methods. By getting the engine and gearbox out in one fell swoop, the removal of the gearbox is facilitated and the tricky business aligning the clutch and gearbox on re-assembly is made much easier.

Before we start on engine removal, by either method, two jobs which are fairly easy at this stage will make things a lot easier later. The first is, simply, to drain off the oil. Do this while it is still hot. The second is only a little more difficult, it is to slacken the crankshaft 'dog' nut (so-called because the dog on the starting handle of older cars used to engage with it) on the front of the crankshaft. Top gear is engaged, and the handbrake firmly applied. It's then just

Above: **Use safe lifting tackle. This 'Spancet' nylon strop carries a tag giving its safe working load in various modes**

Right: **'Clearing the decks'!** Prior to lifting the engine, the battery has been disconnected, the radiator, dynamo, fan, manifolds and exhaust removed, the electrical wires disconnected. Inside and below the car the gear lever, gearbox rear mounting, clutch slave cylinder, propeller shaft and more electrical wiring have been cleared. The lifting 'strop' is in position

a case of applying a suitable spanner and giving it a good heave. If at first it refuses to budge, keep your weight on the spanner and give its shank a good thump with a copper/hide-faced hammer, it'll probably yield at the first or second attempt!

The difficulties with the method of engine removal with the gearbox, are that substantial lifting gear and a pair of tall axle stands are essential as the complete unit is heavy and it has to be tilted to quite a steep angle to come out of the engine bay. To minimize this angle I jack up the rear of the car as high as possible before putting stands under to support it in this position. Continuing, the propeller shaft, speedometer drive, clutch operating mechanism, any electrical connections to the gearbox (reverse

'Up she comes'. A small crane (500 kg) lifts the engine/gearbox unit from the Sunbeam. The rear of the car is supported on axle stands to reduce the steepness of the angle to which the engine is tilted.

lamp, overdrive) and the supporting rear cross member have to be removed, but the cross member must be left in place until the weight is taken on the crane.

Under the bonnet, the electrical connections, controls, and instruments must be removed, identifying the electrics for reassembly. If you aren't sure about the colour coding on the wires, then tie little tags on them so they go back in the right place. Remove the distributor cap and its rotor arm and leads for safety, the fuel line from the pump, and the exhaust system from the manifold. In some instances it is advantageous to remove the manifolds to make the engine slimmer. The radiator should be removed. The front engine bearers can be loosened, bearing in mind that one of them may have to be completely removed to get the engine out.

On some cars the slinging of the engine is made easy when a metal stirrup is fitted to the cylinder head studs and the crane hook attached. In the case of the car in the picture sequence this was not so easy. A nylon 'strop' of a known safe working load had to be arranged around the engine/gearbox unit in such a way as to provide the required angle.

It is necessary to lift the engine, just enough to take the weight, before finally removing the bearers at the front

No. 1 inlet valve fully open. The inlet valve can be identified by 'offering' the inlet manifold up to the engine

and the cross member at the rear. The unit can now be gently lifted and maneouvred up and out, avoiding any collisions with the body. Once the engine is at a sufficient height, pull the crane and its load clear and lower the engine/gearbox to the lowest position possible with the unit clear of the ground so that the crane is stable. The crane can now be pushed to a place where the gearbox can be unbolted and taken off, so that the engine and clutch may then be craned on to a bench to be dismantled.

The alternative method of engine removal, leaving the gearbox in place, is more suitable where only the engine is to be worked on. This method is to be preferred where the job has to be done single–handed, since generally no tilting of the unit is required. The removal of controls, wiring, and ancillaries in the engine bay is as previously described, but the gearbox is unbolted from the engine at the bell housing. Before removing the last bell housing bolts, the gearbox should be supported on a jack so that there is no tendency to bend the gearbox primary shaft as the engine is pulled clear. As before, the engine should be transported on the crane with its jib in the lowest position giving enough ground clearance.

Preliminary checking

With the engine out and on to the bench, don't be in too big a hurry to tear it apart. First take a good look at it.

'Top dead centre' marks on Sunbeam timing cover and pulley

The external state may reveal several 'pointers' to its internal condition. If there is a lot of oil-staining around the oil filler (providing careless filling can be ruled out), or the engine breather, then you should suspect trouble with pistons, rings, or cylinder bores. Rusty water stains might indicate nothing more sinister than a loose hose clip, but there might be a frost crack in a cylinder head or block. Look too, for mutilated threads, broken studs and so on, making a note of them for rectification.

The next move is to take off any remaining 'straight-forward' ancilliaries: starter motor, generator, water pump, oil pressure 'sender' etc, but before you take the distributor out or loosen its clamp bolt, turn the crankshaft until no. 1 piston is at top dead centre, at the end of its compression stroke. To get to this position with certainty, you must, first, locate the inlet valve for no. 1 cylinder. It may be necessary to remove the valve/rocker/camshaft cover so that the valve can be seen and related to the inlet manifold. Now turn the crankshaft, in the normal direction of rotation (clockwise viewed from the front), watching the valve open and then close. At this point the crankshaft is about 140 degrees before 'top dead'. Now turn the shaft until the timing marks or the TDC marks, preferably the latter, are aligned. You now have a reference point to which you can return. Make a simple sketch of the top of the distributor, showing its position and that of the rotor arm. Keep the sketch safe for reassembly.

The distributor can now be removed. If it is driven by an offset tongue make a sketch of the position of that too.

Dismantling the engine
1. Cylinder head and rocker gear
Unless you have an overhead camshaft motor, cylinder head removal is straightforward. In the case of the side valve engine you merely undo the nuts, a little at a time, in a diagonal pattern, starting from the front or rear. It might be necessary to 'break the joint' at the head gasket, by tapping the head sideways and upwards using a hide-faced hammer, or a 'hard' hammer with a piece of hardwood interspersed between it and the head. The head can then be lifted off. In a pushrod ohv engine, it will, most

Offset drive for distributor drive (Jaguar)

likely, be necessary to take off the rocker shaft, before undoing the head nuts. If this is the case and some of the nuts holding the shaft are head nuts, you must undo the smaller auxilliary nuts before those that have a shared duty and must therefore be undone in the proper diagonal sequence. Institute some system to keep the rocker shaft assembly and the push rods in the correct order for putting them back together.

2. Overhead camshaft cylinder heads

Where there is an overhead cam the valve timing must be disturbed before the head is removed. The procedure to ensure correct reassembly varies considerably between makes. Read your workshop manual most carefully. In any case, with an overhead cam engine be certain that you know how to retime it before pulling it apart.

3. Aluminium cylinder heads—difficulties

Considerable difficulty may be experienced when trying to remove an aluminium cylinder head. This is caused by an electrolytic action between the steel studs and the head material with water acting as an electrolyte. It is most serious in side valve engines. In ohv engines where the head studs are within the rocker cover, hardly any trouble is experienced, presumably because oil seeping down between the stud and its drilling acts as an insulator between the dissimilar metals.

4. Sump

Sump removal comes next. This should present no difficulty. If, after you've taken out 'all' of the screws, it still seems tight, it may be that it's just the gasket sticking, *but* it might also be that you've missed an elusive screw somewhere! *Only* when you have made certain that no screws remain, should you resort to 'jarring' the sump with the hide faced hammer to break the joint.

5. Flywheel

The flywheel can be taken off at this stage, to clear the way for crankshaft removal. Ordinarily, this job is straightforward, but some pre-war cars and Leyland front wheel drive vehicles, have a flywheel mounted on a taper on the crankshaft and secured by a single centre bolt, or sometimes a nut. Both the undoing of the fixing and getting the wheel off its taper may call for a bit of serious application.

It's worth taking some time to make up a wooden stand for valve train parts. This stand accommodates push rods, valve springs, valves, spring caps and collets

The more common flywheel, held on typically by four or six bolts and a register on the crankshaft is likely to be much easier. Before lifting the wheel clear, note any markings on its periphery, (typically 1/4, 1/6 or something of that sort) so that it can go back in the same place.

6. Piston and connecting rods—upward removal

In most engines built since the war, the pistons can be withdrawn through the cylinder bores. Check whether this is so by taking off one big end cap and trying it into the cylinder to see if it will go through. Assuming that it is possible, go ahead and undo and remove the remaining connecting rods and pistons, having first ensured that the big end caps, con rods and pistons are marked, unambiguously, so that on reassembly, everything goes back in its correct place. Before you actually push the rods and pistons out, use a bit of 'dead' emery cloth, moistened with paraffin, to take off the ring of carbon that occurs at the top of the cylinder, beyond the limit of piston ring travel. This will also ease any wear ridge that might exist. If the wear ridge is severe, something more drastic may be needed. I would use a bearing scraper, but not everyone has one of these. Without a scraper there's not much for it except persisting with an emery cloth, perhaps using some with a bit more cut in it and a coarser grade. The pistons and rods will, most likely, have to be tapped out using a 2 lb hammer and a suitable piece of hard wood. It's better to apply this to the gudgeon pin bosses within

Above: **On a long stroke engine, like this 2½-litre Daimler, the connecting rod will not pass through the cylinder as demonstrated here using the big end cap—so the pistons and rods must come out through the crankcase**

Below: **Where the pistons and connecting rods come 'up through' a bearing scraper may be used to 'break' the wear ridge at the top of the cylinder so that the rings may pass. (Morris Minor)**

the piston, rather than the con rod.

7. Pistons and connecting rods: removal downwards
Should your engine be one of those which the pistons have to be drawn out downwards, because the rods won't go through the bores, then it may be necessary, certainly it'll be easier, to get the crankshaft out of your way first. Start by getting the timing chain and sprockets out of the way. The dog nut should have been loosened before the engine was taken out. Take it, and the timing cover, off now. After undoing the central nut or the series of screws/bolts that secure the camshaft sprocket to its shaft, the camshaft sprocket together with the crankshaft sprocket and their chain, may be eased a little at a time from their shafts. The big end caps can now be removed, as can the main bearing caps, after making sure that they are marked in such a way that there can be no doubt about their right position on reassembly. The shaft can now be lifted out.

Two difficulties may occur at this stage of the work:
(i) The timing wheels are usually tight on their shafts. They can, usually, be eased off using two broad tyre levers. The levers should apply their force as near to the centre of the wheels as possible, especially on BMC Leyland A series engines where damage will occur if levers are used on the edge of the wheels.
(ii) Main bearing caps are likely to be an interference fit in the crankcase; that is to say, the width of the cap is a little greater than that of the recess in the crankcase into which they fit. 'How' you will ask 'do we get them out?' In almost every case where there is a considerable interference, a substantial tapped hole is provided in the bearing cap. The hole takes a threaded adaptor, to which a slide hammer is attached. It is then a simple, self-evident job to pull out the cap.

With the crankshaft out of the way it is an easy matter to pull the pistons out supporting them with one hand as they emerge. All of the remarks on taking off the timing gear and removing the crankshaft also apply to the other type of engine where the connecting rods pass through the cylinders.

8. Camshaft, oil pump, distributor drive.
With all of the main bits out of the crankcase, there will

Using two levers to ease the camshaft sprocket off its shaft. Apply force near the centre of the wheel to avoid damaging the edge. (Leyland Mini)

remain the camshaft, oil pump distributor drive and, possibly, the tappets (or cam followers). Oil pumps are usually easy to remove, just undo the bolts and pull them out. The associated relief valve plunger and spring should also be removed for inspection. Distributor drive removal should pose no problems, but remember that it must be correctly positioned on rebuilding the engine. If it is of the offset tongue type and you didn't make a note of its position earlier, grab your last chance and make a sketch of its position relative to some datum position of the camshaft, say, when its key slot is vertical. The camshaft can, now, be carefully drawn out, guiding it past its tappets, which are easily pulled out once the shaft has been removed.

Dismantling cylinder head assembly
The parts you have taken out of the cylinder block can, at this juncture, be put into a bowl of paraffin prior to cleaning, while you turn your attention to the cylinder head and valves. If yours is an overhead camshaft, then a good start can be made by taking out the camshafts; on twin-cam layouts, it is essential and while it is not always strictly necessary on all single ohc units its removal might as well come sooner as later, unless there is some constructional feature that prevents it.
Valve removal

A small wire brush in an electric drill is effective in removing carbon from the combustion space as shown or from the valve ports. Don't let the brush come into contact with valve seatings or the cylinders head joint face. (Rover)

Valve removal amounts to compressing the spring, removing the split collets, releasing the spring, and pulling the valve out of its guide; but before doing this, you should make some provision for keeping the valve components and in the correct order for rebuilding. This need be nothing more than a piece of cardboard with numbered holes, but a wooden stand is better. (See page 21.)

The specific tool you need to compress the valve springs will vary with models, the biggest differences being between those for side valve, ohv and ohc. A frequent difficulty, when removing valves, is that the valve springs seem to 'refuse' to be compressed. The problem is not with the spring, but with the collets and the spring cap. The tapered face of the paired collets, with the force of the valve spring applied to them via the spring cap acquires a strong frictional hold on the latter. To break this hold so that the spring can be compressed, put some load on the cap and spring with the compressor and give the forked end of the compressor's 'leg' a short, sharp rap with a small hammer.

Cleaning parts

Before we begin the critical business of inspection and wear assessment, the pile of assorted bits must be cleaned. Methods of cleaning will differ for different parts. Unless the engine was in exceptionally poor condition the flywheel will need no more than the removal of any clutch dust. Because this may contain asbestos, you ought to play safe and *wipe* it off using a rag moistened with paraffin.

Carbon should be removed from the combustion spaces in the cylinder head and from the piston crowns using a blunt scraper. Although it is frowned on in some circles, for good theoretical reasons, I finish these using 'wet and dry' paper wetted with paraffin. A somewhat similar method is adopted for the valves. They are first given a cursory examination, so that time is not wasted cleaning obviously burnt valves. One expects the inlets to be dark grey to black in colour. The exhausts might be anything from a light grey, through a pale, pinkish brown to white. What you are looking for is uniformity in each category.

Exhaust valves 'live' a very difficult life, their operating temperature is likely to be 700–900 degrees C at which

Above right: **Removal of a cylinder head stud in the traditional way. Two nuts are locked firmly together on the stud, as shown here after which the stud may be unscrewed by turning the lower nut. (Sunbeam)**

Above: **This type of stud extractor which employs an eccentric wheel may be simply turned by a 'tommy' bar or by socket set extensions as shown here. This tool is fast and effective at undoing and tightening studs, but may cause some real damage to the stud. This tool covers a range of sizes. (Jaguar)**

temperature they are pounded on to their seats several thousands times per minute by the valve springs. Conditions not unlike those employed by a smith for forging! Getting back to cleaning, once you've rejected any obviously burnt valves, the rest can be prepared by, initially, scraping and chipping off the carbon. Then, with the valve rotating in the chuck of an electric drill, preferably the pillar type, a piece of *worn* emery cloth, wetted with paraffin is held against the head of the revolving valve, taking good care to keep clear of the seating and the stem, until the valve appears shining and metallic all over. If, however, your engine employs aluminium, or other metal-coated valves, abrasives must not be used to clean them as this will destroy their protective covering.

Valve ports are best cleaned using a small purpose-made wire brush in an electric drill. The remaining engine parts can be cleaned in paraffin. At this point, it's a good idea to 'rod out' the oil ways using $\frac{1}{8}$ in. welding rod or something of that size for the purpose. You'll need to repeat this last operation later in the procedure.

Causes of wear: cylinders and crankshafts

Forewarned, they say, is forearmed, so before we begin to inspect the engine for wear, let's try to think about what caused the wear and what its effects might be. Starting with the major units, cylinder bore wear has several causes. One of these is the gas loading on the piston which creates considerable 'thrust' between the piston and the cylinder wall

The cylindrical type of extractor is effective and fast and doesn't damage the studs. A set of tools is needed, one for each stud diameter. (Morris Minor)

during the power stroke. In a conventional front engine, rear wheel drive vehicle, the 'thrust' side of the piston is on the left as you *face* the engine; i.e. on the off side. Another reason for serious bore wear is called 'attrition'. When the piston is in mid-stroke, its speed is high and the piston rings, especially the compression rings, slide over the oil film on the cylinder walls, but at the ends of the stroke the piston stops and the combination of the spring of the ring and the gas force acting behind it squeezes the oil out from under the ring so that no oil film separates the parts and as the piston moves away from the point at which it was stationary, small particles of metal are torn off the rings and the cylinder. This effect is obviously going to be much worse at TDC, where the gas pressure and temperature are a lot higher than at BDC. A third contributory factor in the causes of wear is the chemical attack on the cylinders and piston rings. When the piston stops at TDC and the oil film breaks down, as described above, the upper part of the cylinder wall is left without a film of oil to protect it from the corrosive attack of acids, formed in the combustion process.

When the crankshaft is revolving it is normally completely separated from its bearings by a film of oil. If this film breaks down at all, the failure will take place when the combustion force is applied to the connecting rod. Under those conditions, the centre line of the crank web and that of the connecting rod are almost in line. When the crank web is at 90 degrees to the cylinder axis, the piston is at a speed near to its maximum so that little acceleration or deceleration is taking place and consequently, hardly any force is being applied to the shaft. In practice, it's not unusual for a crankpin or main journal to wear with a taper towards, or away from its centre.

Measurement and wear assessment:
1. Cylinders/Crankshaft

Armed with this information, it seems sensible to take six measurements on each cylinder, crankpin, and main journal to assist us in making the important decision as to whether the cylinder block and the crankshaft are fit for further service without attention, whether a rebore on

The tapered collets securing a valve may be 'reluctant' to yield their frictional grip in the spring cap. A sharp rap with the hammer whilst the valve spring compressor is applied will free them. (Rover)

the block or a regrind on the shaft is needed or whether some more specialized treatment, such as fitting sleeves (or liners) to the block or metal spraying the crankshaft is going to be necessary. For the cylinder bores, three measurements are taken on the thrust axis, i.e. across the engine and three at a right angle to those on the gudgeon pin axis. The crankpins and main journals are measured at a position almost in line with the crank webs and at 90 degrees to them. I use the word 'almost' since, because the maximum gas force is applied to the piston and through it to the connecting rod *just after* TDC, the greatest wear is to be expected to be a few degrees around the pin, or journal, in the opposite direction to normal crank rotation, from the TDC and BDC positions repectively. Since these are important things to be decided upon it's a very good idea to tabulate your readings in order to make an appraisal. Specimen tables are shown overleaf.

2. Stud removal

Before getting down to the practicalities of measurement the studs on the headface must be removed. I like the traditional (and cheap) method of locking two nuts on to the stud and screwing it out. The pictures show two stud extractors. The more expensive cylindrical type does less harm to the studs.

Cylinder measurement table

NUMBER	POSITION	TOP	CENTRE	BOTTOM
1	Thrust axis			
	GP axis			
2	Thrust axis			
	GP axis			
3	Thrust axis			
	GP axis			
4	Thrust axis			
	GP axis			

Note: GP denotes gudgeon pin. The gudgeon pin axis is in line with the cylinder block whilst the thrust axis is at 90 degrees to it

Crankshaft measurement table

NUMBER	POSITION	FRONT	CENTRE	REAR
Crankpin				
1	In line			
	90 degrees			
2	In line			
	90 degrees			
3	In line			
	90 degrees			
4	In line			
	90 degrees			
Main journal				
1	In line			
	90 degrees			
2	In line			
	90 degrees			
3	In line			
	90 degrees			

Note: In line means in line with the crank web and 90 degrees means at 90 degrees to the crank web. Ideally this last measurement should be about 5 degrees from this position in the opposite direction to crank rotation

3. Measuring instruments and some substitutes

There is a difficulty over measuring: the instruments used by a professional mechanic, excluding the allegedly trained finger nail and native wit, will be a high cost external micrometer for the crank and a comparator gauge, sometimes called a Mercer gauge (in the same way as we call our vacuum cleaners Hoovers), to determine the cylinder wear.

There are alternatives to buying expensive instruments:

a) Take your bits along to an engine reconditioner to be measured, bearing in mind that he has a vested interest!

b) An ingenious method of determining the clearance between a crankpin or a journal and its bearing, is to use something called Plastigauge. This is a plasticine-like material which comes in strips of specific thickness and width. In use, it is placed between the bearing cap and the shaft, at various points and at 90 degrees to the length of the cap. The cap is fitted to its rod or to the crankcase, as the case may be, and the bolts tightened. The cap is then removed and the Plastigauge strip, now squashed to a fraction of its original thickness, is taken out and its new, much increased width is compared with a standard which comes with the kit and relates width to thickness and hence the clearance between a shaft and its bearings so that some inferences can be drawn about wear. Really it's easier to use than all that suggests!

c) The alternative to using the expensive but accurate comparator for cylinder measurement, is to use a cheap piston ring and a feeler gauge. The ring preferably new, is fitted into the previously cleaned zone at the top of the cylinder, this is beyond the limits of piston ring travel and should thus be unworn. The ring is 'squared' in the bore by tapping it gently (very gently!) from below using a piston. The gap is measured, the piston ring is now moved to a worn part of the bore, squared as before, and the gap measured again. Remembering that the circumference of a circle is π times its diameter, it will be apparent that the increase in the gap represents π times the increase in diameter. As a practical approximation, dividing the measured difference in gap by three will give the bore wear.

By measuring its deformed width against a scale provided 'Plastigauge' will indicate the clearance between a crankpin or main journal and its bearings. (Jaguar)

Wear limits: cylinders and crankshaft

Having got some measurements, let's consider limits i.e. how much wear is permissible before re-machining. Opinions differ but for car size engines I think:

The maximum crankshaft wear shouldn't exceed 0.001 in. (0.025 mm) and cylinder wear should not be more than 0.2 per cent of its diameter, e.g. about 0.006 in. (0.15 mm) for a typical 3 in. (75 mm) bore car engine.

The maximum oversize to which most engines can be bored is 0.060 in. Crankshaft undersizes don't normally go below 0.03 in. Cylinders worn beyond these limits can be restored by resleeving them—an expensive specialist job. Crankshafts that are outside of limits can sometimes be reclaimed by metal spraying and subsequent re-grinding.

Visual inspection: cylinders and crankshaft

Just as important as all this measuring is a thorough visual check. The crankshaft should not exhibit any appreciable 'ridging' or discoloration as the result of overheating. Look critically at the keyways for the timing sprocket and pulley, the threads for the dog nut and at any oil flinger or return scroll. There is absolutely no point in regrinding a shaft damaged in any of these ways.

The side clearance on the top ring shown here being measured, has for most pistons a top limit of 0.006 in. (0.15 mm) but on this Jaguar piston the limit is set at 0.003 in. (0.075 mm)

Cylinders may have deep 'tramlines' as the result of a gudgeon pin moving out of place, deep rust pitting (especially in an old engine that's lain around outdoors), or be damaged as the result of piston seizure.

Pistons and connecting rods

There is not a lot of measuring to be done on the pistons. About all that is needed is to clean the ring grooves thoroughly, (a broken ring pushed into a file handle is ideal for this) and to check the side clearance of a *new* ring in each of the grooves. Only the top groove is very likely to be worn. More than 0.005 in. or at the most 0.006 in. entails rejection, so that unless you are able to buy over-width rings and get someone to turn out the ring grooves for you, you'll have to buy some new pistons.

As with all engine inspection, a good visual examination is as important as measurement, some minor damage to the crown of the piston by foreign matter can be tolerated, but not any significant scuffing of the skirt, implying a partial seizure. It's not generally possible to buy gudgeon pin circlips separately, in removing them there is a possibility of their being strained or 'pinging' off into the unknown, so I'd advise that unless you've some evidence

Checking a cylinder head for bowing the usual allowable bow is 0.004 in. (0.1 mm) end to end 0.0015 in. (0.035 mm) from side to side in engines of this size. (Leyland Mini)

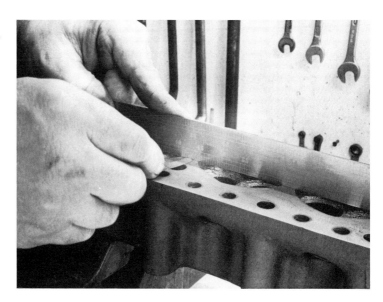

of a fault with the gudgeon pin or the small end bearing, you leave the pistons assembled onto their rods.

Connecting rods are sometimes bent. Abnormal bore wear may be a pointer to this. It is not really possible to test a rod for bending without some special equipment, so if you suspect this trouble you'll have to trot along to a specialist to get him to check them.

Camshaft and tappets

Assessing the camshaft is a comparative process. Plenty of data is available on crankshafts, pistons, cylinders, valves etc.—but camshafts . . . . So, all we can do is compare. This wouldn't be so bad if a new shaft was on hand, but this is seldom the case. What can be done? If you have a suitable 'mike', start by comparing the overall height of the cams. Quite recently, I found a .070 in. variation between cams on an MGA camshaft! It's easy to visualize the effect that would have on performance! Because many cams incorporate quietening ramps, attempting to measure the diameter of the base circle on which the cam is 'constructed' is likely to prove fruitless.

What is going to be more useful is a patient, thorough, visual inspection, looking for signs of uneven contact between the cams and their tappets, any nose circles that have worn to sharp peaks, faint lines across the surface of the cam; sometimes accompanied by a slight colour change in the metal, which indicates that the hard surfacing has worn through, 'sharp' or chipped teeth on the gears for driving the distributor, oilpump, or rev counter and any damage to the key way or threads where its driving sprocket or gear is mounted. The tappets should be free from pitting and any wear marks, (which might be straight or circular). The base of the tappets should, in most engines, be flat. Remember the camshaft and tappets are, to a considerable degree, responsible for 'what it goes like and what it sounds like' and that they are often overlooked.

Camshaft bearings

Camshaft bearings are hardly ever a source of trouble, so much so that in some instances the shaft runs directly in the cast iron of which the block is made. It is therefore unlikely that you'll have to replace them. If you need to, this I'm afraid, is another job for the specialist.

Oil pump/relief valve

The final 'crankcase' item to be checked is the oil pump and its relief valve. The clearance between the pump rotors or gears, between them and the casing body of the pump and the end float between them and the end plate is vital if a satisfactory oil pressure is to be generated. Visually you'll be on the watch for hollowing of the end plate and ridging of the gears or rotors. BMC/Leyland cars in which the engine and gears share the same oil are especially prone to this.

The relief valve plunger and its spring are inexpensive items and might, if available, be replaced as a matter of course. If you can't get them, and the faces of the valve and its seating are suspect, you could try lapping them using fine valve grinding paste, but, if you do this remember that it is *vital* that *all* traces of abrasive are removed. If you are not going to be certain that you can do this it's better to take a chance on a 'dodgy' relief valve than to risk extensive and possibly recurrent damage to major components as the result of grinding paste finding its way round the engine with the oil.

Cylinder head

The 'bowing' of the top face of a cylinder block, where it makes its joint is so unusual to be regarded as freakish, but bowing of a cylinder head is much more common especially where the head is of aluminium. To test the head for bow, the face is thoroughly cleaned using a sheet of emery cloth on a block of steel or hardwood, then a straight edge is placed along the length of the head and at various points across its width. You assess the bow by trying to push a feeler gauge between the head face and the straight edge. The test is then repeated, but this time using the straight edge across instead of along the joint face on the head.

A 'snag' which can occur with aluminium cylinder heads and, much more infrequently with those of cast iron is corrosion of the waterways.

Severe wear on a starter ring gear. (Leyland Mini)

Flywheel

Inspection of the flywheel should not present too much difficulty as only two, or at the most, three, checks are needed. Firstly, the ring gear for the starter motor. The tooth wear will be concentrated in zones which are related to the crankshaft's top dead centre positions, two for a four cylinder, at 180 degrees three for a 'six' at 120 degrees and four for a V8, this time at 90 degrees. Wear extending for more than 20 per cent of the width of the teeth at any of these positions indicates the need a for new ring gear. Don't attempt to fit this yourself. Ring gears have to be 'shrunk' into position, a process needing special skills and equipment and thus clearly the domain of the specialist. Secondly, the flywheel face on which the clutch plate bears may be scored, or show evidence of overheating, possibly in the form of 'blueing' or of thermal cracks. Anything more wrong than light scoring of the face means that the wheel must be scrapped. The third possibility of a flywheel defect is that the spigot, dowels or taper which locate it to the crankshaft may be damaged. You'd be very unlucky to find anything wrong here, but it'd be silly not to check.

Water jackets

If the engine you are restoring has for one reason or another, lain around for some time, especially if it was drained of water, it is probable that the rust and scale deposits, have solidified in the water jacket surrounding the cylinders and in the waterways in the cylinder head. It is imperative that these deposits are removed if the proper running temperature is to be achieved throughout the engine. Remember, local overheating is a prime cause of thermal distortion, this is likely to lead to rapid and uneven wear and perhaps, early failure of parts, especially exhaust valves as the result of thermal stress. Obviously, this accumulation, which has, most likely, assumed the consistency of cement must be removed.

First, the core plugs must be removed. Standard procedure for this is to drive a *sharp* chisel through the plug and then to give its shank a sideways twist;—but be *careful*, the use of too much force could break away a rust eroded recess leaving you with quite a problem! If you have reason

Replacing core plugs after cleaning the water ways. New plugs are used, their recesses being cleaned and then painted with a jointing compound before the plug is sealed in place with *one* good blow at its centre. (MGA)

to suspect serious thinning of metal sections by rust, then play safe! Make sure that the chisel you use is really sharp and before using it drill a line of small holes across the plug so that their edges almost touch. It will then be a much easier matter to cut the weakened plug without damaging its recess.

The next thing is to break up the deposits of scale and rust. Again, attack it sensibly, not too ferociously, prodding it with a soft piece of metal beaten into a chisel shaped tip (aluminium is ideal). Or try perforating it with holes made with, say $\frac{1}{8}$ welding rod tapped with a small hammer. These methods will all help to dislodge the stuff which forms a very effective heat barrier between the metal parts and the water intended to cool them. When refitting a core plug of the Welch type, ensure that its seating recess is thoroughly cleaned, apply a *thin* coat of jointing compound, put the plug in place, then using a good 'solid' drift, give it *one* good firm 'thump' in the centre with a 1 lb hammer

Valve guides

The condition of the valve guides will have a considerable effect on the standard of valve seating you achieve and regardless of that standard, on the subsequent valve life.

Using a hammer and a drift to remove valve guides. If a press is available it is to be preferred for this job

Although valve guide condition is crucial it's rather difficult to make the decision whether the guide is fit for further service. This is because the considerable thermal expansion of the exhaust valve necessitates a large radial clearance when the valve is cold. Furthermore, in effect, guide wear cannot be separated from valve stem wear, fortunately, the latter can be both seen and felt and is one of the criteria to be applied when inspecting the valves.

It is of no help saying 'be guided by experience' if you haven't any. So what can be done? The mechanic with whom I worked as an apprentice used to say that if you put your finger over the end of the guide as the valve was pulled out on the initial dismantling of the engine, and a good 'suction' could be felt the guide was OK. Another angle on this is, logically, look at what happens to the valve and guide when the engine is running. The effect of the rocker, and to a lesser degree the tappet in side-valve and some ohc motors, is to push the valve stem sideways in its guide. The plane of this wear is 'across' the line of the cylinder block or head, so some evidence of wear can sometimes be had by 'waggling' the valve in its guide in this plane and then in one at 90 degrees to it.

After all of this you may still be in doubt, if so it is better to fit new ones, but remember that having done that the valve seatings will need to be trued to the new guides by

Checking the height of the new guide above the cylinder head using a straight edge. (Note drift in foreground). (Morris Minor)

cutting or stoning lightly, a job for the specialist. Fitting a new guide is not, however, on many engines, beyond the scope of the amateur. In many cases the guides are of plain cylindrical form, held in place merely by their interference in the cylinder head. To get these out you need to make up a simple drift, shouldered and with a parallel portion to fit the guide (see photo). This is used with a 2 lb hammer to drive out all but the two end guides. The new guides are driven in, using a straight edge across the original end ones as a depth gauge. When all of the others have been fitted, the end ones may be replaced. If the head is of aluminium or for some other reason the job looks complicated—entrust it to a specialist.

Valve inspection—should they be refaced?

At the cleaning stage you will have discarded any badly burnt valves. Now, a more detailed look at these hard worked parts should be taken. Inlets are the larger ones, it's very likely that they can be re-used, but exhaust valves are a different proposition. You must be very critical in your inspection of these. There should be no signs of serious burning, but some 'pitting' is almost certain to be present. If this is shallow, then you might be lucky and be able to eliminate the pits by the normal valve grinding process. Should this not be the case, then you have a choice

Valves. The exhaust valve on the *right* has quite a good 'land' left above its face. It is unlikely normal grinding in or even a light refacing will alter this

Centre: The valve in the centre has been refaced leaving an unacceptably thin edge to the valve head. In service thermal cracks would be expected

Left: Burnt out exhaust valve

of taking the valves along to a garage or to an engine repairer to get them re-faced, or, replacing them.

If you take up the first option, then, on getting your valves back, check that they haven't been ground out to a knife edge at the top of the seating face. A knife-edge valve will become extremely hot at this outer edge, whilst towards the centre of the valve the temperature may be more than a hundred degrees (Centigrade) lower. This will cause uneven expansion, or, thermal cracking and premature failure of the valve. As though this weren't enough, the seating in the head, or block is likely to suffer some pretty nasty damage, so unless you are really certain about exhaust valves, fit new ones if you can get them.

And if you can't get them? If the valve showed no sign of overheating, and if the valve diameter hasn't been reduced to any great extent, it may be possible to save it by grinding the edge so as to produce a small 'land' parallel to the stem. This will get rid of the problem, but the valve can only be used again if its seating, after 'grinding-in' appears near the centre of the seating face on the valve.

Chapter 3 | # More general restoration

This chapter is mainly concerned with the reassembly of the engine.

Valve grinding

Grinding paste will, in all probability, come in a neat, double-ended tin, containing, at one end 'coarse' and at the other 'fine' emery paste. Forget about the coarse end. If your valves need anything as drastic as that get them refaced. You will need a valve grinding stick, comprising a wooden handle and one, or perhaps two, rubber 'suckers' attached to its ends. The grinding stick is fitted to the valve simply by pushing the suction pad hard against the valve head. If you have difficulty in getting them to hold together, moistening the rubber and making sure that the valve head is free of oil or grease will help.

Valve grinding. After applying a *thin* layer of fine paste to the valve some paraffin (just a little) will improve the speed of cutting

Smear fine grinding paste, thinly, around the seating face on the valve. Then I like to dab a little paraffin on to the paste with my finger. This gets rid of some of the stickiness of the paste and allows it to cut faster. For the actual grinding of the valve, the grinding stick is moved between the palms of the hands like an old-fashioned egg whisk. After, say, ten or 12 movements the valve is lifted, turned a quarter of a turn and the process repeated until, after three to five minutes you notice, from the change in the sound that the 'cut has gone out' of the paste. At this point the valve is taken out, the grinding paste wiped off both the valve and its seat and the faces are checked; but before discussing this two important points should be made:

1. It is not possible to use a valve grinding stick for all valves, on some engines you use a broad bladed screw-

Valves are ground in using valve grinding stick with a movement similar to that of an old-fashioned egg whisk

driver or a special tool with two pegs which engage in two holes in the valve head. In these instances a small spring beneath the valve will help with the lifting of the valve after every ten or 12 grinding movements.

2. Never use a power drill to grind valves; the backwards and forwards movement is essential to produce a smooth all-over seat without circumferential grooves.

Checking and reassembling valves

Most books will say that when the seating faces on the valve and in the head or block are a matt grey all over this indicates a satisfactory condition. Personally, I like to go a little further than this. There are several ways of checking the condition of the seat:

1. Apply a thin 'wipe' of 'engineer's blue' to the valve, having made sure that it and its seat are absolutely clean, drop it into place, turn it through about 90 degrees and back again, there should be a smooth, thin, even coating on each. A good substitute for engineer's blue can be made by holding a lighted candle under a sheet of glass. The deposited soot is then mixed with a *little* light oil.

2. Make marks in pencil around the seat in the head or block at, say, intervals of 20 or 30 degrees. Again, place the valve in position, rotate it through 90 degrees and back. All of the pencil marks should have been rubbed out.

3. This method is more time consuming than the others but it is a thorough check. The valves and their seatings are thoroughly cleaned with a rag, which should be immediately disposed of so that abrasive paste cannot find its way into an engine. The valve stems should be lightly oiled, and the previously cleaned springs cap and collets refitted. The head or block is then laid on its side and the ports are filled with paraffin. Over a period of, say, three minutes, there should be *no* leakage into the combustion chamber. If the result is satisfactory, the valves may remain in place. If not then there must be further grinding and testing until the result is satisfactory.

Two more points about the assembly of valves. Don't

forget to fit new seals to the valve stems if they were there originally. It may be that only the inlets are so equipped. It's sometimes difficult, with the valve springs compressed, to fit the collets and then keep them in place whilst the spring is released. The job can be made easier by smearing a little grease onto the inner radius of each collet to hold it in place. The best grease to use is water pump grease.

Building crankcase assembly: preliminaries

With the valves reassembled into place, attention may be turned to the rebuilding of the crankcase assembly, the major part of the engine. It cannot be stressed too strongly that great care must be taken to rid the engine of swarf, grinding dust, valve grinding paste and other abrasives left after machining or other processes. It's also likely that the engine's 'arteries' are clogged with a build up of carbon and oil residues. Clearing the oilways in the crankcase and the crankshaft is, like the previous work on the water jackets, unglamourous but vital if you want to build long life as well as performance into the engine. If the crankcase oilways are closed by screwed plugs (often they have socket heads to take Allen keys) they should be taken out and they, together with those in the crankshaft, should be 'rodded' out. I find $\frac{1}{8}$ in. welding rod useful for this. I suppose aluminium is ideal but I doubt that steel will, in practice, do any harm. After rodding, flush through the drillings with paraffin. If you have a source of compressed air at your disposal, use this to clear out the paraffin which will otherwise dilute the vital engine oil prior to the first start. If not you'll have to just do the best you can by energetic use of a hand or foot pump! After this the crankcase should be thoroughly internally washed and then dried. Although some makers do it, I don't believe in painting the inside of engines as dislodged paint particles could cause trouble in the lubrication system.

With most of the dirty work behind us we may now contemplate the building of the crankcase with some pleasure. Unless there is some good reason to the contrary (like non-availability) you should renew piston rings, big end and main bearing shells and all gaskets as a matter of principle.

Assembling the centre main bearing thrust washers. In all engines it is vital that the thrust faces are of bearing metal. In some instances they can be fitted the wrong way round with potentially disastrous results. (MGA)

Fitting crankshaft and pistons

Whether you fit the pistons and connecting rods next, or whether you start by fitting the crankshaft, will depend on whether the big ends of the con-rods will pass through the cylinders. If they will, the crankshaft goes in first and if not the pistons and rods take priority.

Let's follow the first possibility:

1. The upper housings for the main bearing shells should be wiped clean and dry. Before fitting, the size markings on the back of the shell bearings (usually at one end near the locating lug) should be checked to see that they correspond to the size of the shaft. Satisfied about that, seat the top half shells into their housings by hand. See that the little locating lugs are properly engaged with the slots in the housings. At this stage I smear the bearing faces with a little clean engine oil, but some people prefer to use a graphited preparation like Graphogen.

The crank-shaft can at this stage be lowered gently into place, keeping it level and trying not to allow it to turn. Next fit the upper half thrust washers. It is possible to make a serious mistake here. Be very certain that these are assembled with their 'bearing' metal faces towards the crankshaft. Getting this wrong might prove very expensive. Wipe out the housings for the lower half shells in the main bearing caps, seat the shells 'home' as before, oil the shells and lower thrust washers and fit the caps and thrust washers into their correct places, tapping the caps home with a copper hammer if necessary. Lightly 'nip' the main bearing nuts up and check that the shaft revolves freely and smoothly. That being the case, use a torque wrench to tighten to the figure recommended by the manufacturer. This is important. Once again make sure that the shaft turns easily and smoothly.

2. Fitting pistons from crankcase

On some engines, usually those having pre-war origins in the UK, the small cylinders will not allow the big ends to pass. In quite a lot of these engines it *is* possible, albeit with some difficulty, to fit the pistons and con-rods after the crankshaft, but even if this is the case, it is easier to fit the rods and pistons first.

A few engines made life really difficult because the

In some cases there is a considerable interference between the main bearing cap and the crankcase so that the caps have to be hammered home using an copper hammer

pistons had to go in from the top (cylinder head) face of the block but the connecting rods had to be fitted from below. Sometimes, this entailed starting the piston, fitting its skirt ring, pushing the rod up from below and then aligning the small end eye and the gudgeon pin bosses so that the pin could be fitted! If yours is one of these engines you'll need all the patience and dexterity you can muster!

We'll suppose though, that the task facing us is the easier one of fitting the rods and pistons from the crankcase side. When the pistons go in from below, there is often a generous 'lead' or chamfer on the bottom of the bores so that, in some cases, the pistons can simply be pushed into the cylinders without having to use any sort of piston ring clamp.

Where the pistons and rods are to be fitted from below and there are shell bearings, leave the shell out of the rod until the piston is in the cylinder. Should you have the earlier, direct metalled bearings then it's probably best to temporarily fit the big end caps to protect the bearing while the piston is started into its bore. If you are going to attempt to fit the pistons without recourse to a ring clamp: I stress that you need a really good chamfer at the bottom of the cylinder to make this possible.

3. Gapping piston rings

You must first of all, check the gap of your new rings when fitted to the cylinder. Place the ring in the cylinder and using the piston with no rings on push or tap the ring very gently, to 'square' it in the bore. The gap can now be checked using a feeler gauge. Follow the engine or piston makers' recommendations as to gap, but if none is available, you'll be fairly safe in using 0.003 in. per inch of cylinder diameter for compression rings; unless they are chrome faced, when you should allow another 'thou' per inch. Oil control rings of the slotted type also need about 0.004 in. per inch of diameter. Steel rail rings are pre-gapped. If the gap is too small, file the end of the ring carefully to increase it.

After gapping the rings, go back over some of your earlier work making sure that the ring grooves are quite free from carbon. Check that with a new ring no groove has more than a maximum of 0.006 in. side clearance. The

Checking the ring gap the piston ring is 'squared' in its bore using a piston and its gap is measured with a feeler gauge. (Rover engine)

rings can now be fitted. Few professionals use any aids for this, but if you are inexperienced you might find it helpful to use three 'slithers' of thin sheet steel to ease them into place. Now stagger the ring gaps at even, angular intervals around the piston. The cylinder bore and the piston should be very generously oiled. Work the oil into the ring grooves by pouring it into the gaps and rotating the rings en-bloc around the piston.

Inserting the piston entails lining it up with the bore in both planes having taken cognisance of any 'front' marking and having made sure that the ring gaps are well clear of any cut-outs to clear the conrods, pushing the rod firmly but gently home. Where there is little or no chamfer on the bottom of the cylinder bore, you will need a piston ring

Fitting pistons and rings. In this picture a piston and connecting rod is being fitted from below into the side valve engine of a Morris Minor MM. No ring clamp or compressor is needed since the generous taper on the bottom of this bore and pre-gapped piston rings make things easy. Nonetheless a last minute check on piston ring positions and a good oiling with SAE 20/50 oil is needed before fitting, which is a case of keeping things square and pushing the piston and rod into the bore

This picture shows how three thin steel 'slithers' help in manoeuvring the piston rings into place without breakage. (Sunbeam engine)

clamp (skirt, compressor) to enable you to start the rings into the bore. The procedure is pretty much as before so far as ring gapping, setting, checking of side clearance, lubrication and the staggering of gaps is concerned. The clamp will keep the ring gaps closed, but in doing so will set up quite a frictional force between the piston and the clamp. Because of this you will probably have to tap the piston/con rod assembly into place. I find the shaft of a 2 lb.-hammer ideal for this. Take good care that you don't tap on a bearing surface.

If you've fitted the pistons from below, you can go ahead and fit the crankshaft following the general instructions given before. If, on the other hand, you've been able to fit the crankshaft first the pistons and rods may now be fitted from above. You will, of course, still have to check the ring gaps and side clearance and lubricate and stagger the rings. Where a piston entry is from above it is important that the rings are clamped as tightly as possible by the clamp as it's very unlikely that there'll be any chamfer at all to help you start the piston rings. The pistons will have to be tapped on their crowns with a hammer shaft as previously to take them into their bores.

If during this the piston is felt to stop, it's a near certainty that an insufficiently clamped ring is unable to enter and is abutted against the top face of the block. In any case as soon as the piston stops you *must* investigate the cause, making sure that the rings aren't damaged. In all of this reassembly work it is *essential* that the parts go back into their correct places and that they are fitted the right way round.

In case you've forgotten how things go a little help can be given. If a piston has a split skirt then that, in a conventional engine layout, goes to the near side of the engine and if there is a small drilling in the connecting rod to direct oil on to the cylinder, this will go to the off side.

With the pistons all started and the crankshaft in and its main bearing caps tightened, the big end shells and caps may be fitted, following the same sort of procedure as for the mains, tightening them progressively to the correct torque, fitting any locking devices and ensuring that the engine remains free to turn at each stage.

Fitting a piston from above. In this MG Midget engine the cylindrical piston ring clamp contracts the rings into position as the piston is tapped home using a hammer shaft

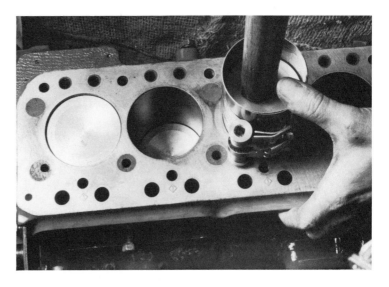

For the moment let's assume that the camshaft in your engine is situated low down in the cylinder block/crankcase assembly, the most common position, that all is well with the camshaft bearings and that the decision to replace the shaft, or not to, has been taken, the tappets and camshaft can be oiled and placed back in position. Most likely the camshaft will be chain driven. As with shell bearings and piston rings, timing chains should be replaced 'on principle'.

In this instance it is permissible to fit a new chain on to worn sprockets. Sprockets are seldom hooked to any extent and chipped teeth almost unknown. Of course if either of these faults is present both wheels should be replaced. If you put the old chain back it is likely to spoil both the sound and the performance of your newly rebuilt engine. The performance would be down because the effect of the stretch of the chain is to increase the length of the chain run from the crankshaft sprocket to that on the camshaft, thus retarding the timing of the camshaft.

It is very unlikely that there won't be timing marks on the sprockets. Typically, they are marked with 'ls', 'Os' or 'dots' and it is necessary to line these up on a line passing through the centre line of both shafts. Many modern timing chains are of the endless type. With these it is obligatory to place the wheels within the chain and with the timing marks aligned, turn the camshaft and the crankshaft until their keys are in the right positions and then to push the assembly home. If the valve timing isn't marked on your engine or you want to experiment with different timings then refer to the chapter on 'nasties'.

Front pulley timing cover and oil seal

Before you refit the timing cover you must renew its oil seal. The traditional felt type might give rise to a little difficulty. The trick is to soak these in engine oil, to make them supple before fitting and after fitting, to ease the front pulley through the seal in the cover, line up its keyway and *push the pulley and cover into place together*. This last point is good for almost all timing covers and pulleys, whatever seal is employed (providing the seal in the covers encircles the shaft). Fitting the pulley and cover together is especially pertinent to engines where an oil return 'scroll' is employed at the front of the crankshaft. With the pulley fitted the crankshaft dog nut, or screw, can be lightly nipped up. Final torqueing up can wait until after the flywheel is fitted so that it can be employed to lock the crankshaft.

Refitting oil pump

Earlier in your overhaul, you will have inspected the oil pump. On some gear pumps a considerable improvement in their performance is to be had by the simple expedient of grinding the end plate flat using some valve grinding paste smeared on a piece of plate glass. The end plate is rubbed on this with a circular motion applying some downwards force to keep the face flat. This 'dodge' is worth considering if yours is a gear pump and replacement items are unobtainable. It's likely to be of less help on rotor and vane type pumps and *should not* be used where there is aluminium or other soft metal used for the end plate because of the likelihood of abrasive material becoming embedded and consequently, making things worse rather than better.

Before fitting the pump, fill it with oil, some may, subsequently leak out but that which remains will help to ensure that oil reaches the bearings as quickly as possible.

Timing marks: In this case 'dot' markings between the crankshaft and camshaft sprockets. In re-assembly a steel straight edge is used to check that a line 'drawn' through those centre punch dots will pass through the centres of the shafts

Timing distributor drive

The upper part of the shaft which drives the oil pump may also drive the distributor, so it might be necessary to locate this shaft in some specific position to facilitate the timing of the distributor later on. You should have made a sketch of this on dismantling. If you didn't refer to the chapter on 'nasties'.

If a separate shaft is used to drive the distributor this can go in next referring to your sketch for its correct position.

Sump and oil strainer

The oil pump will have a separate coarse strainer, after having a final check on your crankshaft bearings to be sure they are torqued properly, any locking devices are fitted, that the engine turns reasonably easily and the strainer is clear. The strainer and the sump may be refitted.

1. Rear engine plate

There may at this stage, be a rear engine plate to be attached. The plate serves to mount the starter motor and the gearbox bellhousing.

2. Flywheel

The next major item to be put back is the flywheel, but, before doing so, you ought to make sure that the spigot bush (or, sometimes, a bearing) in the back of the crankshaft is fit for further service. This little component could be the source of a lot of bother if it proved to be faulty after the engine and gearbox were refitted into the car. Fitting the flywheel only entails checking that it is correctly positioned (remember you checked its marking when dismantling?) and seeing that it is right 'home' on its mounting register before tightening its bolts to the correct torque and fitting any locking device there may be.

3. Water pump

Bolting the water pump (discussed in the chapter on cooling) back into place is the last job before re-uniting the cylinder head with the rest of the engine.

Fitting the cylinder head

Jointing compounds with gaskets? If it's for a cylinder head, then, generally I'm agin' it; the exception being the case of the copper and asbestos gasket now quite uncommon, which might benefit from being smeared with water pump grease—otherwise I'd always assemble head gaskets dry. For the rest I won't be dogmatic, but if you do use a compound I'd advise a fairly liquid one rather than the 'gooey' variety.

Studs—cylinder head and gasket

Refitting cylinder head studs is a reversal of the dismantling procedure. Be certain that the studs go back in their correct places, there may be several different lengths, that the threads are clean and sound before fitting and that they screw right home. Ease the gasket over the studs to avoid 'wrinkling' it as it slides into place. Give each bore one generous squirt of engine oil from your can, take a last look into the cylinders and at the head face to see that all is well, and then lower the head into place.

Tightening the head

The head has to be tightened progressively. Most manufacturers will have published an order of tightening. This may not be the case for some of the oldest cars, or you might not have the information— in either instance you'll generally be safe in working diagonally outwards from the centre, taking the nuts down to the correct torque in three or four stages.

Setting valve clearances

Whether the head is torqued down before the rocker shaft is fitted will depend on whether the rocker shaft pedestals are held down by head studs. With the push rods inserted into their proper place and rocker shaft assembled and tightened, the valve clearances may be given their initial setting. It is very important to ensure that the tappet, which in most cases you can't see, is resting on the back of its cam which in all probability you can't see either! This doesn't, however, constitute a big problem. Because there is a 360–degree crankshaft angle and, hence, a 180–degree camshaft angle, between specific events, say power strokes, in specific cylinders, we are able to use this knowledge to ensure that any particular valve has its tappet resting on its cam at the lowest point on its profile. This is essential if the adjustment is to be done properly.

When no. 1 cylinder is at TDC on its firing (or power) stroke, no. 4 in an in-line four-cylinder engine will be beginning its induction stroke 360 degrees away. It follows that when any valve on no. 1 cylinder is fully open, the valve which fulfils the same function on the opposite no. 4 cylinder is fully closed. Cylinders two and three are 'paired' in the same way, half a turn out of phase with one and four. To make sure the 'rule of nine' is 'invoked' where there are four cylinders, adjusting no. 8 valve while no. 1 is fully open; 7 with 2 fully open, and so on. A 'rule of 13' is used where there are six cylinders in line. The lock-nut on the screw at the end of the rocker is undone, and the adjusting screw is tightened until a feeler gauge of the correct thickness is just 'nipped' between the rocker and the valve. The screw is then *slowly* undone until the gauge will just slide out. The locknut is tightened and a final check is made to ensure that the clearance is correct.

Once the valve clearances are set, pour about a quarter of a litre of oil over the valve gear to give some early lubrication after the first start. Fit the rocker cover, using a new gasket and tighten it down. Valve clearance adjustment on overhead camshaft engines will be dealt with later.

Restoring your engine appearance

Opinions vary as to whether it is better to paint the engine while it is in small parts, or to wait until it is all assembled. I take the latter view. By this time the engine will be fairly clean but it can be improved upon before painting by using an old (but not too old) nail brush with some paraffin to scrub the dirt from the pores of the castings. Follow this with rotary wire brushes on your drill and then some emery cloth for as long as you have the patience, to get the castings as smooth as possible. I find that hand painting, using perhaps a $1\frac{1}{2}$ in. brush for the bigger expanses and a $\frac{1}{2}$ in. one for the more fiddly bits and heat resisting engine paint gives a good but not over-restored look. Paint is available in makers' original colours.

Polished aluminium castings add the finishing touch to an engine's looks. In restoring once-shiny castings from a corroded state you may have to progress through a file (but gently), fine emery cloth, wetted with paraffin, wet-and-dry paper, also paraffin wetted, burnishing compound ('T' cut or the like) metal polish, and finally, silver polish. It is of vital importance that in all of this dusty work with abrasives around that all entries into the engine are blanked off—or many hours of improving 'what it goes like' and 'what it sounds like' will have been lost in carelessness in improving 'what it looks like'.

Preparation for storage

If the engine is not going to be installed more or less immediately, all of the ports should be blanked off using masking tape. About a quarter of a litre of oil is shared between the four spark plug holes and old plugs screwed in in an attempt to prevent corrosion.

Some afterthoughts

1. Wet linered engines

These are generally thought of as a high quality alternative to the normal engine construction in which the cylinders are directly bored in the crankcase/cylinder block casting. They are used by makers such as Aston Martin, AC and Alfa Romeo as well as by the manufacturers of more mundane vehicles such as Renault and the former Stan-

Wet liner construction. A Triumph TR engine sectioned to show the liners their spigots into the crankcase and their lower seals. This is an 'open deck' wet liner construction

dard Motor Company, who used this construction in their Vanguard engine and in its derivatives used in the earlier Triumph TRs and Morgans—to say nothing of Ferguson tractors!

The main advantages claimed for this method of construction are longer life, better cooling and ease of servicing. The disadvantages, apart from the higher first cost, are centred around the problems of keeping the lubricating oil and the coolant from invading one another's 'territory'. Cylinder wear is seldom a difficulty and, if it does occur, the cylinders can, in many instances, be merely pushed out of the crankcase by hand and new ones put in in the same way. If they can't be pushed out, it's generally possible to tap them out using a block of hard wood and a hammer. A word of warning though!—some liners have a thin brittle bottom edge which be damaged if you hammer it. In these instances you'll need to draw the liner out. A disc is necessary, having a shoulder turned on it to fit inside the bottom of the liner. It should have a hole at its centre through which is passed a long piece of, say, $\frac{3}{8}$ in. diameter rod— long enough to pass up through the cylinder, plus about three inches. A 'U' shaped bridge—2 in. or so deep—is placed over the rod so that it spans the top of the liner and bears on the top of the cylinder block. By fitting a nut to the rod and screwing it up the liner will be withdrawn.

When fitting wet liners, especially if there was evidence on dismantling of water getting into the oil, or vice versa, be certain that the seating faces for any gaskets or O-rings are perfectly smooth. It is also of prime importance that the liners protrude above the top of the cylinder block by the specified amount; this dimension is laid down so that the necessary high pressure joint at the top of the liners is obtained. With wet liner engines it is crucial that cylinder head tightening is done in accordance with the makers' instructions.

2. Making it go a little faster

Most enthusiasts seem to want to make their cars go just that little bit faster, so I'll offer a little advice. The intention is not to do anything very drastic at all, leaving valves, camshaft etc. in their standard condition, but doing a little better the things the manufacturer did in a hurry for economic reasons.

All of this work is on the cylinder head and manifolds, so obviously, it should be carried out before the head assembly is put together and fitted.

With the valves still out the ports should be smoothed using whatever tools are most convenient. Rotary files in an electric (or air powered) drill are likely to prove very useful, but for some of the difficult bits you'll find it necessary to use hand scrapers and perhaps strips of emery cloth held over the blade of a small screwdriver. Little is to be gained by going beyond smoothing the ports and polishing them.

The inlet manifold can, often with considerable advantage, be matched to the cylinder head. First of all you should establish whether there is any positive alignment between the head and manifold. Where the manifold is held by bolts their necessary clearance may build in quite a lot of latitude! If you have this problem then you'll need to dowel the intake manifold to the head. A possibility here is to get two special studs made up to replace the end bolts—these might incorporate concentric dowels. Providing there was enough 'meat' around them, the holes in the manifold could be carefully enlarged to provide a positive location. Do not dowel exhaust manifolds or thermal cracking may result.

Once you know that the manifold is always going to take up the same position in relation to the head, you are in a position to match them to one another. Both jointing faces must be flat, clean and smooth. (Bowed inlet manifold faces are frequently a source of unstable idling and poor performance.) One face is next smeared with engineer's blue or home-made marker paste as described previously and the head and manifold bolted together. On taking them apart the mismatch on one side will be apparent and can be corrected using hand or rotary files. The procedure can now be repeated, except that this time the other component is marked.

The combustion chambers in your engine may have been left 'as cast'. If this is the case it's a good idea to smooth them without altering their shape. This done, and with the valves fitted, measure the volume of each space and then by *carefully* removing metal with your rotary files, match the volumes of the smaller ones to that of the largest, measuring the volumes with paraffin poured from a pipette calibrated in millilitres (or cm³). It's a good idea at this stage to calculate the compression ratio:

Compression ratio: $CR = \dfrac{Vs}{Vc} + 1$ where Vs is the swept vol. of one cylinder and Vc is the clearance volume

Vs can be easily calculated using $Vs = \dfrac{\pi}{4} \times b^2 \times s$ where b is the bore and s is the stroke

(I'd suggest that you work in centimetres so that Vs comes out in cc [more accurately cm³]—a familiar unit).

Finding the value of Vc is probably best done empirically. With the engine on the bench and the cylinder head

removed, one piston is placed as accurately as possible at
TDC and its edge is sealed to the cylinder wall using water
pump grease—pushing it right into the small space
between the piston and the wall. The grease must not protrude above the top of the piston. The head is fitted next,
with the valves fitted leaving the pushrods or camshaft out
and using a gasket. It is then tightened. *During the fitting
of the head the crankshaft must not be allowed to turn.* The
engine is now positioned so that the spark plug hole is
vertical and using the calibrated pipette the combustion
chamber is filled with paraffin to the bottom of the spark
plug hole; some care is needed over this. By subtracting
the volume left in the pipette from that with which we
began we will have the volume necessary to fill the combustion space = Vs, so that we can calculate CR.

Knowing what the compression ratio is we can next consider raising it a little to make best use of the fuel which
is available today but may not have been when many 'classic' engines were built. It must, however, be borne in mind
that future legislation might force the anti-knock value of
petrol down again.

With an ohv engine, with or without overhead camshafts, you ought to be able, safely, to aim at a ratio of 8.5–
9.1 on today's fuel.

By transposing the formula we can fairly easily arrive
at the value of Vc which will give us the compression ratio
we want to use.

$$CR = \frac{Vs}{Vc} + 1 \quad \therefore \ CR - 1 = \frac{Vs}{Vc}$$

$$\therefore \ Vc = \frac{Vs}{CR - 1} \quad \therefore \ \text{If } CR = 9 \quad Vc = \frac{Vs}{8}$$

Subtracting the 'new' Vc from the original we will know
the volume to be taken out of the combustion space. Now
volume = area × depth so by dividing the volume by which
we want to reduce Vc by the area of the combustion space,
we will have obtained the amount to be machined off in
a value which a machinist can use. Our remaining difficulty
is to obtain the area. I suggest rubbing a fairly soft pencil
over a piece of graph paper placed on the head and count-
ing the number of small squares enclosed by the diagram.

Multiplying this number by the area of one square will give the total area. Dividing the volume by this will tell us how much we must get skimmed off the head.

Chapter 4 | A conventional four-cylinder pushrod engine

For the first of our case studies I have chosen the Sunbeam Alpine engine. It is a straightforward four-cylinder unit of $1\frac{1}{2}$ litres or a little more. It is thus a contemporary of the very popular MGA/MGB and Triumph TRs. The whole car represents, in many ways a good restoration prospect.

The engine like the BMC 'B' series unit is a family car engine mildly 'worked over' to raise its power output from, say, 50 bhp to about 80. Because of its relationship to all of those family cars and the large number of common parts, the spares situation is not as difficult as it might be.

Dismantling the Alpine engine turned out to be fairly straightforward. If you've absorbed chapters 2 and 3, one of these engines isn't going to give you a lot of hassle.

There's a side-plate on the Alpine engine. Some people, when doing a top overhaul, merely undo the bolts going through the plate and into the cylinder head and slacken those which go into the block in a vertical line. They then ease the plate and its gasket away from the head, using a steel rule or something of the sort. Whilst this 'dodge' is useful when time is short, since it avoids the necessity to disturb the oil filter base or distributor, it is, however, slightly dubious because unless great care is taken the gasket may be damaged, resulting in an oil leak. Since, in this instance, the object was to do a complete strip of the engine, I took out the distributor, first setting no. 1 piston on TDC, as described in chapter 2, making a sketch of the distributor base relative to the engine's block and the position of the rotor arm for reassembly purposes and took off the oil filter base and the side plate.

Unlike the standard Hillman engine, which is its an-

Dismantling the Sunbeam Alpine engine. With the No. 1 piston set at top dead centre at the beginning of the power stroke (see chapter 2) the rotor arm was in this position relative to the distributor body and the engine. A note was made of this in the form of a simple sketch before the distributor was removed

After removing the distributor its offset drive was in this position. A sketch was made of this too. It would be needed on re-assembly

cestor, the Sunbeam engine sports a nice polished rocker cover, which looks well and, held down by four $\frac{1}{4}$ UNF studs, is quite oil tight. According to the type of spanner you use, you might need to take some care to avoid scarring the cover. The rocker shaft comes off in two halves, but before you can do this, the oil feed pipe which goes into a brass fitting between the two halves, must be removed. You'll need a $\frac{3}{8}$ in. AF spanner for this. Sensibly, the rocker shaft is held down independently of the cylinder head bolts and studs so that its removal doesn't entail taking note of the cylinder head nut sequence. Once I had got the rocker shaft off I could concentrate on the head.

My engine had been sitting on the bench for more than a week, so there was no need to worry about it distorting as the result of heat—remember aluminium heads, like this one must be stone cold before dismantling. Because this engine hadn't done much work since it was last 'down', I had none of the difficulty that sometimes happens when removing aluminium cylinder heads.

After I'd got the head off, I took out the two long studs at either end of the block face on the near side. This isn't absolutely essential but it helps in three ways: the block face may be thoroughly cleaned up using a sheet of emery cloth on a steel block, the engine can be stood on its head face to take off the sump and remove the crankshaft and its associated bits and finally, when fitting the pistons and rings, during reassembly one has clear unobstructed space in which to work.

There are one or two points about the timing cover and the camshaft drive which are worth noting. The oil 'sealing' of the cover, where the crankshaft emerges, is by that time-honoured device the oil return scroll (it is also employed at the rear end of the crankshaft). Because of this, you'll need to take some care to centralize it on reassembly, there is also an oil 'flinger' which keeps a lot of the oil away from the scroll. It is important to put this back the right way round. A small screw in the centre, carrying a fibre washer can easily be missed when undoing the cover, especially if the engine is 'caked' in road dirt (clean it first!)

Within the timing chain cover there's a little oil pipe to

Before the rocker shaft could be removed, its oil supply pipe ($\frac{3}{8}$ in. AF spanner) had to be disconnected

Crankshaft pulley oil return scroll. Care has to be taken on re-assembly to centralize it in the timing cover

supply the chain from the main gallery. To remove it I held the bigger head with a $\frac{1}{2}$ AF spanner while the smaller one was undone with a 4BA spanner . . . much kinder than pliers!

The chain tensioner came off easily, removing the split pin with side-cutting pliers, but both the crankshaft and camshaft sprockets were fairly tight on their shafts and needed a firm pull with two 'substantial' tyre levers to remove them. The way was now clear to remove the front engine plate, once the cylinder block drain pipe was taken off. The special extended bolt, for the screw in the centre of the cover was also taken out at this point.

Before the camshaft could be taken out, the tappets (or as some will have it; cam followers) had to be removed. This proved to be a source of some difficulty. They should just pull out of their guides in the cylinder block, but they just came up flush with the top and no further. I've had this trouble before, the usual cause is oxidized oil forming a deposit on the lower, crankcase end of the tappet, effectively increasing its diameter. In the past I've got over this

The chain tensioner pad on 'our' Alpine engine was badly cracked as well as worn out

This little pipe lubricates the timing chain. A 4 BA and a ½ AF spanner are needed to remove it. See that its oil holes are clear

difficulty by shaping a piece of softwood into a long taper, hammering it *lightly* into the tappet so that it wedges and then after a generous dousing with releasing oil to soften the deposits, lifting and turning the tappet until it comes free. There is a possibility of splitting a thin walled tappet when using this method, so I substituted my second finger for the piece of wood and with some perseverance they all 'freed up' and came out. I was then able after removing the sump and the oil pump, to take out two retaining bolts and their plate and withdraw the camshaft.

The flywheel was undone. The bolts were tight (as they should be!) Their torque necessitated jamming the flywheel teeth with a tyre lever and the application of a good 'heave' with a socket and a long sway bar; but before this could be done I had to bend back the lock plates using a small hammer and a chisel. There was no need to mark the flywheel on this engine for reassembly, as there is a dowel which ensures that there is only one position in which it can be put on. The main and big end bearing caps were undone, a little at a time, parts were laid out in their correct order. I lifted out the shaft and retrieved the thrust washers which fell into the crankcase as the shaft came out.

After I'd removed the upper big end shell bearings, I pushed out the connecting rods and pistons with the cylinder block supported on blocks of wood so that it was horizontal. As each piston emerged I supported it with my left hand to avoid damage to it or its rings. The 'front' marking on the pistons were cleaned and the pistons numbered for reassembly.

What conclusions did I arrive at before embarking on measurement? Well, I'd expected the engine to be in fairly sound condition and this had been largely, confirmed as stripping proceeded. About all that I'd found up to this point was some totally unexpected and heavy corrosion around the thermostat and its housing, some worn tappets, a worn out timing chain tensioner pad, and one slightly chipped oil scraper ring on no. 4 piston. I was disturbed to see on the big end shells, which were fairly new signs of uneven 'bedding' and since they bear no identifying numbers, I suspected that the caps might have been assembled on to non-matching rods—a problem.

The tappets were tight in their guides. The photograph shows how they were turned and lifted after a thorough soaking with WD 40 oil

Method of jamming the flywheel. In this case to tighten its bolts. To undo them the lever would need to rest on the bottom of the starter hole

Measurement and inspection

Crankcase assembly and cylinder block

Apart from the points already noted as defective, what did I find when I got down to measurement? The major measurements revealed little cause for concern. The cylinder bore wear wasn't at any point more than 0.0035 in. As an authority on bore wear limits I draw on Sir Harry Ricardo, respected for his experimental work on aero marine and road vehicle engines, who suggested that there would be no significant loss in engine performance until the cylinder bore wear exceeded 0.2 per cent of the cylinder bore diameter. In the case of the Alpine engine, this would set the bore wear maximum at approximately 0.0065 in., so my cylinders were well inside of the limit.

The pistons were in good condition with a maximum side clearance of 0.002–0.003 in. on a new top ring. This top piston ring side clearance is a most important measurement on any engine. To disregard an excessive clearance— say more than 0.006 in. here means you're likely to finish up with broken rings and irreparable piston damage.

Crankshaft wear was low at 0.0007 in. maximum on the crankpins and rather less than that on the mains, well within safe limits.

The oil pump clearances were 0.006, 0.005 and 0.002 in. for the outer rotor, inner rotor tip and end clearance, against the limits of 0.008, 0.006 and 0.003 in. respectively, so this unit too was deemed suitable for further use.

The crankshaft and bearings were in good order, so all in all it looked as though this would be a low budget overhaul.

Cylinder head assembly

Alpine engines suffer from corroded waterways. As the metal is eaten away the water holes get nearer to the edge of the combustion spaces until a leakage occurs. First symptoms of this are often excessive water loss with no external leaks, signs of discharge from the radiator vent pipe and oily scum floating on the water in the 'rad'. In the case of this engine the head had been welded some three years ago, so was found to be in good condition. A picture has been included showing a badly corroded example from another Alpine to warn readers of what to expect.

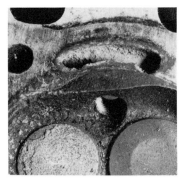

Not, fortunately, from our engine but showing clearly how a corroded water way in an Alpine engine can break through into a combustion space. A specialist weld, refacing and drilling would make it re-usable

Bright marks on inner valve springs show where they've rubbed on the outers as the result of 'bowing'. Remedy, fit replacement springs

I've already mentioned the heavy corrosion of the water outlet and thermostat housing. When I took the thermostat housing off, I found that although there were no water leaks this component was cracked. This was repaired by an oxy-acetylene weld, the face being 'trued' with a file.

Both inlet and exhaust valves, the rockers and their shafts were in good shape but the inner valve springs showed bright marks on some coils caused by rubbing on the outers whilst bowing under load, so they had to be replaced.

As expected, bearing in mind the difference in operating temperature, the clearance in the exhaust valve guides was greater than that for the inlets, but neither gave cause for concern.

Assembling the cylinder head

Once the valves had been cleaned using a pillar drill (as described in chapter 2) they were ground in. The seating face on the valves and the corresponding face on the inserts were easily restored to good order. The valve stems were lightly oiled before re-assembly and new O-ring oil seals were inserted into the valve caps before assembly. These are not very obvious (see photo), and can easily be over-looked. If they aren't replaced excessive oil consumption is likely to result.

With the valve springs and collets back in place and the valves 'bounced' off their seats using a tyre lever to ensure that the collets were properly 'home' in their tapers on the valve spring caps. The completed cylinder head was put on one side to be fitted to the cylinder block/crankcase assembly later.

Crankcase/cylinder block assembly

I guessed that reassembly would be a fairly straightforward business, and straightforward it turned out to be. In the main it was a reversal of dismantling, ensuring that everything was adequately oiled as it went together. Surprisingly, main bearing thrust washers for the Sunbeam engine are not, as is frequently the case, supplied with the main bearing shells. Measurement of the crankshaft end float (with the centre main bearing cap off and the others bolted up) indicated 0.007 in. of travel, whereas the limits are 0.002–0.004 in. Fitting a new set brought it back to

Ensure that these plates are in position before fitting the valve springs

The valve spring cap is shown here resting on its rubber seal. The seal is fitted into the bottom (nearest) end of the cap. To neglect oil seal replacement may lead to excessive consumption

My favourite piston ring clamp. See text

0.002 in. I've included pictures showing the use of 'professional' equipment in the form of a dial test indicator and a magnetic base to measure end float as well as the humble feeler gauge. Whichever method you pursue, you'll need to push the crank firmly forwards and backwards to the limits of its movement using a lever, to ensure that you measure the entire travel.

The assembly and progressive torquing down of the main bearing caps was straightforward except that initially the front of the no. 1 cap which forms part of the joint face for the front engine mounting plate wasn't flush with the front of the cylinder block which forms the other part of that face. There is some lateral freedom on the bolts which could, unnoticed, lead to an oil leak. What I had to do was to loosen the bolts and the cap, tap it forward as far as I could and down into position, and temporarily assemble the front plate to hold everything in place while the main bearing bolts were tightened to their proper torque. With this done, the flywheel was fitted and tightened to 40 lb. ft.

In inserting the pistons, it's essential to check that the front markings are forward and the appropriate crankpin at its position which corresponds to bottom dead centre. If you are using a piston ring clamp of the same sort as the one I used (see photo) be careful to see that the bottom edges of all of its parts are exactly the same height. If you

The professional way. Measuring crankshaft end float using a dial test indicator and magnetic base

The perfectly sound diy alternative using a feeler gauge at the centre main. Whichever measuring instrument you use it is essential to use a lever to ensure that the crank moves to its limits forwards and backwards

don't, a ring can easily 'escape' and be broken as the piston is tapped into the cylinder bore.

As each piston was fitted and each bearing assembled the engine was turned, checking for free rotation—a slight drag from the piston rings in mid stroke is acceptable.

When fitting the front engine plate only a few bolts, which do not go through the timing cover can, at first, be fitted. In the past I've had some difficulty in 'starting' the remaining bolts when fitting the timing cover, so now I fit *all* of the bolts which go through the front plate temporarily into place to ensure that subsequent assembly is possible without damage. I then tighten those which do not go through the timing cover and remove the others. Remember to fit the little oil pipe that feeds the chain.

Fitting the timing chain

The camshaft was inserted with six replacement tappets and two sound originals, and secured by its plate. The engine was turned so that nos. 1 and 4 pistons were at TDC and the camshaft turned to the corresponding position with the cams for no. 4 cylinder 'equally downwards'. A check was then made that the dot punched timing marks on the sprockets were aligned with each other and through the centres of their shafts.

It's necessary to start the crankshaft sprocket first and

On initial assembly to front main bearing cap was about 0.012 in. (0.3 mm) out of position (see text)

to tap it onto its shaft for about an inch and a quarter with the camshaft wheel and the new chain hanging on it. At this point the camshaft wheel could be eased on to its shaft making any necessary small adjustments to the shaft or the wheel to ensure that the keyway in the sprocket and the key on the shaft were in alignment and that the two 'dot marked' teeth were in their proper places. With the camshaft sprocket started over its shaft, it and the crankshaft sprocket were driven home. I stopped tapping the camshaft wheel just before it was right home and pulled it finally into place with its securing screw which was then locked with a plate.

Before going on to fit the timing cover, tensioner and pulley I turned my attention to refitting the oil pump and the shaft which drives it with the distributor from the camshaft. First I turned the engine in its normal direction of rotation, (i.e. clockwise viewed from the front), through *one* complete turn, noting from the position of the cams that no. 1 cylinder was 'firing' that is to say, its two cam peaks were pointing equally downward whilst those of no. 4 were now pointing equally up. The oil pump and its drive were inserted so that the latter assumed the position it occupied prior to dismantling. Note that due to the action of the helical teeth, the shaft will turn slightly as it is pushed home. It is its final position that is important. Before leaving the oil pump its coarse strainer which was badly obstructed (see picture) was cleaned using a wire brush and paraffin.

With the pump tightened into place and its delivery pipe refitted I gave the crankshaft bearings, cylinders, pistons and camshaft a generous squirt of oil from below and set about the task of fitting the sump. It can prove difficult to get a properly oil-tight sump on these engines, there being a number of points in this area to watch. Curved seals are used over the front and rear main bearing caps. There are two thicknesses of sealing strip, a thick one for pre-1962 engines and thin ones for later ones. At the time of the changeover (1962) those main bearing caps needing thin seals bore the letters A, B or C.

The sealing strips must fit *over* the gaskets which in turn go onto the flat machined surface of the crankcase. The

a

b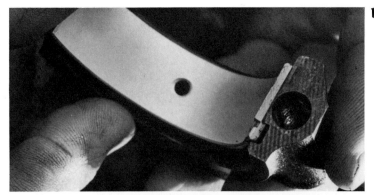

Fitting a shell bearing. A big end is shown. The procedure for main bearings is similar:

a The seating for the shell is wiped quite dry.

b The little lug (bottom right) is engaged with its groove in the cap. (This serves to locate the shell bearing during assembly only).

c The shell is pushed down into place

d The oiled bearings are assembled with their locating lugs at either end of the crank pin but on the same side

c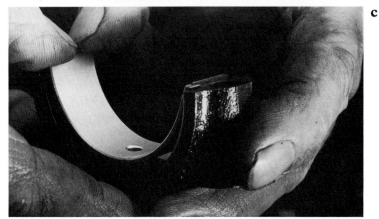

d

The coarse strainer for the oil pump was badly obstructed

gasket must therefore engage the grooves for the curved seal on the outer surface of the main bearing caps. For this purpose little tags are provided on the gaskets. I had some difficulty in getting these tags into their grooves.

Using a sump screw with a substantial *plain* washer in each of the holes nearest the main bearing caps to stretch the gasket into position I eased the tags on the gaskets into their grooves and cemented the sealing strips onto them using 'Uhu' adhesive which was allowed to set. After a careful final internal cleaning the sump was lowered on to the inverted engine and progressively tightened using a $\frac{7}{16}$ AF socket and speed brace. To complete the job the two side stays that brace the engine to the lower part of the bell housing were attached. As the sump was tightened I was pleased to see that the curved seals were properly compressed. It's not too difficult assembling things properly on a clean dry bench with a clean engine upside down. Doing it from below with an oily engine in situ is very much 'a horse of another colour'!

At this stage I could contemplate fitting the cylinder head. The first step was to ensure that the mating faces of the head and block were flat and clean. To this end they had been rubbed with a machined steel block $5 \times 2 \times \frac{1}{2}$ in. ($125 \times 50 \times 13$ mm) and a piece of emery cloth. After lubricating the top of the cylinder bores the head was dropped into place on a dry gasket. The slight latitude on the two

An important detail that needs watching. The thinner main bearing cap seal is for post-1962 engines (see text)

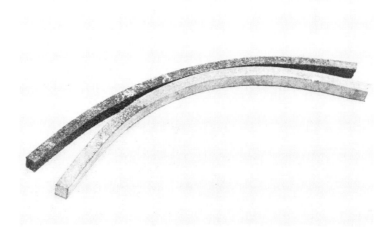

Above: **Trouble with replacement gaskets. Too short to reach the groove in the main bearing cap**

Above right: **How I got over it. Stretched, glued (with UHU adhesive) and temporarily bolted into place**

locating studs of the head was used to ensure that the joint face for the side cover was flat across the junction of the head and the block. Before the head was tightened the oil feed pipe to the rockers was attached at its lower end and the side cover was fitted using a new cork gasket. The head could now be tightened progressively to a torque of 48 lb ft in the sequence shown in the diagram. After fitting the push rods the two half rocker shafts were fitted inserting the oil feed between them and starting its union fitting before the rocker pedestals were finally tightened.

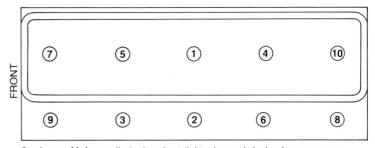

Sunbeam Alpine cylinder head nut tightening and slackening sequence. Torque 48 lb ft.

The valve clearances may be adjusted cold to 0.012 in. inlet and 0.014 in. exhaust (0.3 mm and 0.35 mm respectively). On the first setting after reassembly I like to give each adjusting screw a tap with a light hammer in case small bits of carbon or whatever should prevent the push

The main bearing seal must go over the gasket which in turn must be 'home' in the groove on the cap. These engines are prone to leakage here unless care is taken over these points

rod going right home into its tappet or the adjusting screw into the push rod.

Some Rootes engines like this Alpine unit have a somewhat unusual valve sequence front to rear: Exhaust, inlet, exhaust, inlet, inlet, exhaust, inlet, exhaust, in place of the more common: Exhaust, inlet inlet, exhaust, exhaust, inlet, inlet, exhaust.

From a theoretical point of view this should give improved exhaust valve cooling. From a practical standpoint the 'rule of nine' (see chapter 3) can still be used for valve clearance adjustment, but you must be certain about which are inlets and which exhausts. Once satisfied about this part of the job the rocker cover was fitted as soon as possible as a precaution against anything accidentally falling into the engine.

The distributor was fitted next using a new rubber O-ring followed by the oil filter base, taking good care in the latter case to select the correct gasket from three fairly similar alternatives in the set.

I was now able to return to the timing cover about which one or two points need to be watched on reassembly. These are principally to do with the oil scroll which is used as an alternative to the more usual oil seal. The pulley has to be inserted through the cover to centralize it so that it doesn't 'bind'. To try to mantain a clearance all round (there isn't much room) and to provide some intitial lubrication I smeared a little thick high melting point grease at the root of its horizontal part where it abuts the vertical face taking good care to prevent it entering the groove of the scroll. A new chain tensioner blade and rubber pad were fitted. I greased the rubber pad to prevent it burning on the chain before any oil reached it.

With the oil flinger correctly located (see photo) the pulley and cover were fitted together easing the tensioner pad and blade into the cover with my fingers at the same time keeping the gasket in position—a little tricky! With the cover home all of the nuts and bolts and screws holding it were tightened except for the small $\frac{1}{4}$ UNF screw which goes through the cover behind the pulley. It was necessary to withdraw the pulley to fit this screw and its fibre washer, but this could now be done with confidence since the other

screws were holding the cover in its centralized position. The pulley was now fitted "for keeps" with its dog screw locking plate and locking tab.

The cast–iron engine parts were painted with matt black engine paint and the pressed steel parts were done with black enamel, as was the engine mounting plate. 'As cast' aluminium parts were brushed clean but the rocker cover was polished using silver wadding polish. The fuel pump and valve port openings were blanked off for storage using masking tape. The clutch was fitted and centralized and the gearbox attached. The unit was put into storage to be united with the chassis at a future date. The servicing of the thermostat and water pump will be dealt with in chapter 8.

Above: **Before the timing cover was fitted, the chain was oiled and the new tensioner pad greased. This lubrication is essential to 'look after' these parts until oil reaches them from the lubrication system when the engine is first started**

Above right: **It's important to fit the oil flinger this way round or the scroll on the pulley may not be able to cope with the volume of oil so that a leak occurs**

Chapter 5 | An aluminium alloy vee eight

The Rover engine—dismantling. With eight cylinders to deal with you don't want to get into a muddle over ignition timing. With No. 1 cylinder set to top dead centre at the beginning of the power stroke the rotor arm of the distributor for the P5B and the engine in the Morgan Plus 8 will be in the position shown above

Some Rover V8s e.g. in Range Rovers had the No. 1 position 45 degrees anti-clockwise from that shown above. In either case the rotor arm turns clockwise and the firing order is 1843 6572. Nos. 1357 cylinders are on the nearside and 2468 on the offside

The Rover V8 engine based on a Buick design has proved, over almost 20 years since its introduction, that it possesses a very desirable combination of high torque, smooth running and low weight; the latter being due to the extensive use of aluminium in its construction. The smooth running is inherent in V8s with cylinder banks at 90 degrees to each other. The compact dimensions of the unit have led to its installation in a number of Buick-Oldsmobile models in its original form and in the Rover version to some traditional British sports cars such as the Morgan Plus Eight, plus, of course, in a wide range of Rover saloons and the Range Rover. Additionally, it has proved popular as a custom car transplant engine.

Well, what sort of a restoration proposition is it? The short answer is not a bad one. It is of course an aluminium engine so all of the normal caveats about these apply, especially:

a) Don't disturb any joints with the engine hot.
b) Do always use a torque wrench where figures are quoted.
c) Check joint faces for flatness whenever the engine is dismantled.

In fact you might need as many as three torque wrenches. *Don't* try to improvise or cut corners.

The guinea pig engine was *very* oily and dirty externally, around the cylinder heads and the timing cover, but there was no sign of excessive oil leakage from the rear main bearing seals, popularly considered to be a weak point on this engine. A mental note was made to investigate these leaks as the job proceeded. At some time in the engine's

The distributor base and the aluminium timing cover were 'dot marked' for re-asssembly using a centre punch

history a water pump replacement had been carried out as evidenced by the great amount of gasket cement which had oozed from its joint on to the timing cover. When I took off the exhaust manifolds the exhaust port for no. 7 cylinder (near side rear) was a shiny black suggesting that largish quantities of oil were reaching the combustion chamber—another mental note to search for a cause.

Taking things off in earnest began with undoing a small plate below the back of the sump which blanked off the drive plate, ring gear and torque converter; this unit having come from an automatic car. The next item was the cast aluminium bell housing. I was now able, working from where the small plate had been removed, to undo the torque converter and remove it. Rather a lot of dirtier than usual automatic transmission fluid ran out of the converter after it was removed and the appearance of the whole unit seemed to imply neglect over a long period.

The sump was drained and whilst there wasn't an acute shortage of oil that which was there felt 'thin' and gritty suggesting that it had been a long time since it had been changed. At this stage I left the drive plate and ring gear in place but I did, before turning to the front of the engine, remove the starter motor. I found the bottom bolt a little tricky. At the front of the engine I set about undoing the rather tight bolt attaching the pulley to the crankshaft. With a friend locking the drive plate to the casing a good heave on the sway bar and the socket undid the bolt, after which only moderate force was required, using two tyre levers, to draw the pulley from its shaft.

The power steering pump was removed and after taking off the fan pulley I was able to get the belt for the pump out of the way. Because I was curious I dismantled the water pump and found within some rather nasty signs of corrosion.

Apart from remembering to remove the little flame traps between the rocker box and the carburettors, and to take off the bypass pipe from the thermostat housing to the water pump (a clip had to be sawn through here) the removal of the intake manifold was pretty straightforward. One bolt was just a little awkward. It's just in front of the offside carburettor, but a thoughtfully provided screw-

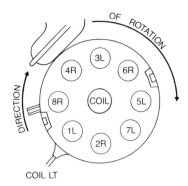

The Rover P5B layout is shown.
Firing order, 18436572. On some Rover V8
applications all of the plug leads are
displaced 45 degrees anticlockwise from
the positions shown

**Distributor cap looking down
onto it**

driver slot made its undoing easy once it had been initially slackened using an obstruction wrench. With the manifold off a rather unusual, thin, curved piece of steel which acts as an intake manifold gasket-cum-tappet cover is revealed. As well as the manifold bolts, two gasket clamps secure this odd component. Removal of the intake gasket laid bare a tappet chest full of black treacly sludge. This reinforced my earlier suspicions of neglected oil changes, or maybe that a faulty coolant thermostat, allowing the engine to run too cold was responsible for the mess.

In preparing to take off the timing cover it became necessary to remove the distributor, so I identified no. 1 lead (nearside front) and traced it back to the distributor cap. Next I undid the spring clips and released the cap so that I could check inside which electrode was connected to the no. 1 lead. Having done this it was a simple operation to turn the engine in its normal direction of rotation, so as to align the metal segment on the rotor arm with the position of no. 1 electrode in the cap so that I had a datum point to which I could return on re-assembly.

I didn't mark any of the other spark plug leads, really there's no need to. With no. 1 lead identified, knowing the

**The timing cover was a little tight
on its dowels. To get it off without
bruising the soft aluminium
cover I tapped the steel plug over
the oil pressure relief valve**

On removing the timing cover it was immediately obvious from the way in which the timing chain sagged away from its sprockets that it was badly worn and would have to be replaced

firing order (1-8-4-3-6-5-7-2) and that the distributor turns clockwise as seen from above, everything can be put back in its proper place. To be able to reposition the distributor as accurately as possible without recourse, intially, to electrical methods, I gently 'dot' punched the distributor body and the adjacent water pump body. By undoing its clamping fork it was then easy to lift out the distributor.

The oil filter canister was spun off and the water pump removed, but before the remaining bolts were undone, the engine was set with no. 1 piston at TDC on its firing stroke, using the pointer on the timing cover and the markings on the pulley.

The cover could now be removed, remembering to take out two, not very obvious, bolts passing through the front of the sump. It proved necessary to lightly, tap the head of the plug over the oil pump relief valve to free the cover from its dowel. The camshaft bolt was undone and the skew gear for the distributor together with the fuel pump eccentric were taken off the shaft, noting the 'F' marking (front) on the latter. Before removing the timing wheels and their badly worn chain I noted that the timing marks in the form of a small arrow on the camshaft wheel and an 'Θ' inscribed on the crankshaft wheel were aligned.

As I got on with taking things to pieces, and removed the rocker covers I found even more sludge, to such an extent that two cylinder head bolt heads on each side had disappeared into a black morass. This part of the work, to say nothing of the subsequent cleaning, was rather unpleasant.

With the heads off there was no evidence of burnt valves or excessive oil consumption. I came to the conclusion that the appearance of no. 7 exhaust port which I mentioned earlier was due to nothing more than the engine having been run for some time with a fouled spark plug!

Once the heads were out of the way I was able to turn the unit upside down and remove the sump and guess what—more sludge! Apart from this, with the sump, its baffle and oil strainer removed, the connecting rod bearings and those for the main journals were quite straightforward to get at. After undoing the appropriate big ends,

This picture shows just how dirty the Rover engine was inside, I ascribe this to short runs and neglect of oil and filter changes

On dismantling, the cause of a lot of oil leakage was revealed as badly fitted rocker cover gaskets. On reassembly they were glued in place

using an ordinary $\frac{1}{2}$ in. AF socket on the special bi-hex. nuts, I tilted the engine to bring each bank of cylinders into a horizontal plane and pushed the pistons and connecting rods out. I numbered the pistons before removal using a number stamp and marking each piston crown just in front of its axis. (It's unwise to mark near the edge because of possible distortion of the top piston ring groove.) The connecting rods have a little boss on their shanks and an arrowhead formed on their caps; these face forward for the right-hand cylinder bank and backwards for those on the left, so that the marks point towards each other when both rods are assembled into place.

The position of the main bearing caps except no. 5 are identified by number and an arrow pointing forward, the position of no. 5 the rearmost, is self evident. The crankshaft thrust is controlled by 'cheeks' on no. 3 main. The caps were tapped lightly to free them and then wriggled out. No. 5 cap and upper bearing housing were sealed by a very old-fashioned method using a graphited textile material—probably asbestos cord. With the main bearing caps removed it was an easy matter to lift out the crankshaft looking rather dirty and a little scored on its 'mains', although all of the bearings were in sound condition. Once the shaft was removed the main bearing caps and shells were bolted loosely back into place.

Attempting to remove the tappets I ran into the same problem as I'd experienced with the Sunbeam; that they were lacquered with carbon below their wear zone and wouldn't come up out of the guides. In this case it was possible to get them up to their limit, draw out the cam-

Inspection wear assessment. The camshaft was badly worn. Note the convex peaks of the cams and their pitted surface

shaft and then gently tap them out downwards. I was reluctant to draw them up through since these are hydraulic tappets and this might instigate a troublesome oil leak.

As the camshaft came out it was immediately apparent that this iron shaft was in poor shape, with the peaks of the cams rounded off in elevation and heavy wear on their flanks. The camshaft bearings were, however, in good shape. The tappets which should be flat bottomed, were very concave and in one instance the surface was beginning to break up. Exploring wear in the valve train a little further revealed a great deal of wear on the rocker shafts and on the aluminium rockers. It turned out subsequently that the rocker oil feed drillings in the heads were just about blocked with the aforementioned sludge and other assorted muck!

Inspection—crankcase assembly

Once the crankcase assembly was cleaned a psychological battle seemed to have been won! I could now take some measurements and introduce some precision into a process which until now had been a dirty struggle. The crankshaft showed a maximum wear of 0.001 in. on the main journals and 0.0005 in. on the crankpins, although there was some light ridging on the journals. So far as the cylinders were concerned, the dry liners were glazed but after 48 measurements showed no more than 0.002 in. wear, so clearly no reboring or indeed other major machining was needed.

Reproducing the convex shape of the worn cams the tappets were worn concave. The picture shows an old tappet on the right and a new one on the left

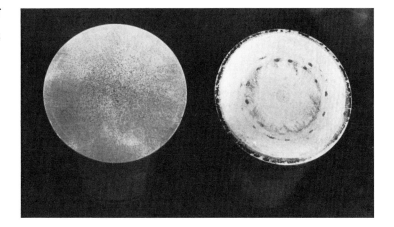

The camshaft bearings as noted before were in sound condition, and the cylinder block to head face was in good condition and free from distortion.

Inspection—cylinder heads

There were no burnt valves and all exhibited fairly good seats with no burning or pitting evident. No. 1 cylinder inlet valve turned out to be slightly bent (see below). The valve guides gave me cause for some deliberation. The exhausts particularly seemed a little slack, but since the slack was all round and not in one plane, bearing in mind the high thermal expansion of the exhaust valves, and because the valves exhibited good seats, I decided against replacement. The head faces were flat and free of scores or serious waterway corrosion, and all threads were in good order, as were the faces for the inlet manifold and gasketless exhaust manifolds.

Reassembly—crankcase assembly

This followed the general lines as described in chapters 3 and 4 being extra careful to avoid damage to aluminium joint faces. The graphited seal for the rear 'main' had to be put in with some care smoothing it into place with a hammer shaft. The maker's workshop manual said it should be rubbed until it was protruding 0.031 in. above its housing—I ask you! The '31 thou' *had* to be an educated guess! It is, however, important to get this somewhere near

Valve operating train wear
extended to the rocker shaft and
to its aluminium rockers

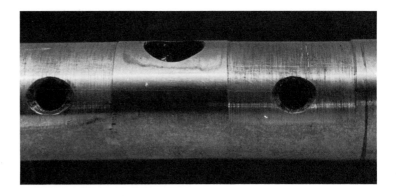

right. Leave it too high and you'll burn the new seal out in the first few revs. Rub it down too far and you've a leak, which to cure will call for removing and stripping the engine all over again. . . . Before the crankshaft was installed this seal was freely lubricated with an SAE 50 engine oil.

So far as the crank itself was concerned I dealt with the ridging of the main journals by polishing them with OO Grade 'flour' cloth (a very fine emery cloth) using the diabolo method, i.e. passing a strip of cloth over the pin and pulling the ends alternately. This done and bearing in mind the generally dirty condition of the engine an extra assiduous cleaning was given to the drillings in the crankshaft—they needed it!

The main bearing shells and journals were generously oiled with SAE 20/50 engine oil and the shaft was gently lowered into position to avoid damage to the rear seal. The main bearing caps and lower shells were fitted observing their numbered sequence and forward pointing arrows. Special shells with 'cheeks' or flanges on them to control end float were fitted to no. 3 main. The caps were all tightened progressively to 50–55 lb. ft except for no. 5 which had to be tightened to 65–70 lb. ft. I was then able to check the crankshaft end float using a feeler gauge at the centre main and levering the shaft first in one direction and then the other. The recorded clearance was 0.005 in. (limits 0.004–0.008 in.)

Next I turned by attention to the pistons. Satisfied that a new piston ring had 0.003–0.005 in. side clearance in the top ring grooves I decided to retain the old pistons and fit new rings.

My usual technique for the very important operation of getting the ring grooves absolutely clean is to break an old ring and use it as a scraper. Now everyone who has built an engine is probably aware from bitter experience just how brittle piston rings are; imagine my surprise when the first ring I tried to break bent—and bent—and bent. This, however, proved to be something of an odd man out. The others broke! Before the pistons were fitted an emery cloth lap was used to 'glaze bust' the cylinders so that the new rings could 'bed in' in a reasonable time/mileage. Using an electric drill on a *slow* speed the lap was moved up and down the bore with quick bold movements so as to produce a cross hatched pattern. I used a plier type ring compressor on this engine. It proved convenient and a bit quicker to use than the clamp type.

Before I started to insert the pistons and connecting rods I'd checked that the crankshaft turned smoothly with just a little drag; so as each rod was fitted I turned the shaft over to check for any excessive increase in drag. I found I was able to insert the upper big end shells into the rods before fitting the pistons and that they stayed in situ as the rods and pistons were tapped into place with a hammer shaft. This made things easier than trying to site the shells with the rod in the crankcase. I checked that my marks on the piston crowns were forward, that the markings on the pairs of connecting rods and their caps faced each other, and that there was the proper side clearance between the rods sharing a crankpin. Rover specified 0.006–0.014 in., 'our' engine had about 0.008 on all pairs. The big end nuts were torqued to 35 lb ft.

With no oil pump or distributor drive to be fitted in the crankcase, I attached the sump temporarily so that the engine could be stood the right way up for the operations of fitting the camshaft, its tappets and the timing chain.

I used a replacement camshaft kit comprising camshaft, hydraulic tappets, rockers and rocker shafts. Of these, clearly the camshaft and tappets had to be fitted to the crankcase. I took some trouble to ensure that every tappet moved freely in a rotational sense as well as up and down.

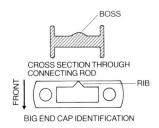

CROSS SECTION THROUGH
CONNECTING ROD

FRONT

RIB

BIG END CAP IDENTIFICATION

Rover connecting rod markings. (LH cyl. rods). Boss on shank of rod-facing back, as is rib on cap. RH rods have their identifying marks facing forward so the marks on adjacent rods face each other

Rod end/big end cap identification

The cause of some of the trouble was an oil drilling in the cylinder head which was almost entirely chocked with deposits

From that time on each new tappet was kept matched to its allotted guide. If the tappets on these engines do not rotate freely, rapid wear and noisy operation are likely to result.

The new iron camshaft with its all over black finish (except for the bearings) looked a little strange to my old-fashioned eyes. Despite this it rotated freely and the tappets followed it very smoothly.

Next, the large Woodruff key had to be transferred from the old shaft to the new one. I 'started' it using a soft drift by tapping down on the end of the key nearest the end of the camshaft which was temporarily placed in the crankcase for support. Once the other end of the key started to come up, the shaft was removed from the engine and the key was gripped firmly in a vice and pulled out. After dressing off a few resulting burrs with a fine file, the key was tapped into place in the new shaft, once again supporting it in the crankcase.

The next task was to fit a new timing chain. In this engine, of US origin, an inverted tooth or 'Morse' chain typical of American practice is used. A long life is claimed for these chains, but in this engine a new one was very necessary. To time the camshaft, the no. 1 piston is placed at approximately TDC—you'll get within 10 degrees either

Rebuilding. The rear main bearing seal is of a graphited material. This is smoothed into its groove using a hammer shaft. The aim should be to obtain an 0.031 in. 'stand proud'. This photograph show the upper (crankcase) seal. When the lower seal, which goes into the cap, has been fitted the curved seal (but not the side seal) has to be cut off to length using a really sharp knife. Later engines use neoprene seals

So that the piston rings would bed quickly, the glaze on the cylinder bores was broken with this emery cloth lap (see text)

way without much difficulty judging by eye when the piston is at the top of its travel. The camshaft wheel is then fitted lightly into place without the chain and turned until the arrowhead timing mark (it actually looks a bit like a church door!) is at the bottom of the wheel and pointing upwards. It should now be aligned vertically with the ⊖ mark on the crankshaft wheel, now at its highest point. Once you are happy about this, both wheels can be slid off their shafts, inserted into the chain and then slid back together into place. The fuel pump eccentric (with F-marks facing outwards) and the skew gear to drive the distributor follow the camshaft wheel on to its shaft, locating over the key. The thick plain washer and set screw are then fitted and tightened to 40–45 lb ft.

Servicing and assembly—cylinder heads

As with the crankcase, care was necessary to avoid scarring the soft aluminium joint faces. To this end a *small* decarbonizing wire brush was used in the electric drill to remove carbon from the combustion space. Good care was taken to keep the drill under close control because if it slipped across a finished face a 'bought out' refacing operation, costly in time as well as money, could be necessary.

After cleaning the valves I got down to grinding them in. They turned out to need very little grinding—with 16 of them it was fortunate. A minor difficulty occurred with the inlet valve of no. 1 cylinder. As the matt grey ground face began to appear it seemed not to follow the machined face on the valve exactly. Some professional equipment had to be brought to bear. The valve was set up in a lathe and turned slowly by hand with a dial test indicator against its head. This revealed a 'run out' of 0.007 in. confirming my suspicion that the valve was bent. Since the error was relatively small the valve was refaced (using a garage re-facer) and having ascertained that there was still a reasonable land above the face, it was reground.

The valves were fitted in the ordinary way and the cylinder head jointing faces were lightly cleaned using 360 wet and dry paper, paraffin wetted. The new rocker shafts were assembled with new straight iron rockers in place of the angled aluminium items originally fitted. The use of

The new tappets were all oiled and checked in their guides for free movement. Tappets and guides were then kept matched for assembly later

The tappets moved very smoothly on the new camshaft. Compare its condition with the worn ones on page 76

straight rockers is facilitated by using wider rocker pads to make contact with the valves. The old aluminium pedestals were refitted as were the spacer rings. I've no quarrel with this.

However, four new split pins in the kit and four new wave washers, since these wear, would also be very acceptable. These additions would avoid frustrations and annoyance, especially for the DIY man without a well-stocked garage stores on hand.

Servicing and fitting the timing cover

On a V8 engine it is common to find the ancillaries clustered around the front of the engine since any components at the side would be made inaccessible by the cylinder blocks and heads. In this case, the alternator, power steering pump, fuel oil and water pumps and the distributor are all ahead of the cylinder block, (adding substantially to the engine's length). Of these, only the alternator is not mounted on the timing cover.

The water pump was found to turn freely with no slack in the bearings or signs of leakage, so this was subsequently refitted as the cover was fitted to the engine.

The two principal jobs around the timing cover turned out to be servicing the oil pump and fitting a new timing cover oil seal.

The heavy oil pump components tend to 'unbalance' the cover in the mechanic's hands, and make it a little awkward to deal with on the bench, so I took this off first. The oil pump came off using a $\frac{5}{16}$ in. AF ring spanner on the

Timing chain, crankshaft and camshaft wheels were fitted. Note the timing marks and the 'F' (front) marks on the fuel pump eccentric. The camshaft bolt is tightened to 45 lb. ft

The angled aluminium rockers were replaced with straight iron ones. This was possible because the contact pad for the valve stem was a good deal wider

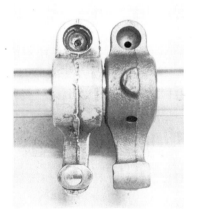

special bolt heads and I took the gears out. The driving gear was a little difficult to remove because the shaft that drives it from the distributor was heavily lacquered with burnt on oil, increasing its diameter and preventing it passing through the cover. However, the application of some WD40 dissolved the build up and after a few minutes 'wiggling' it came out.

I put the oil pump parts to one side and turned my attention to the front oil seal. This is one of the graphited textile type using a similar material to that of the rear main bearing seals; this seal is different though, in that it is in one piece and is retained in place by a shaped aluminium ring 'staked' into its recess in the timing cover by three centre punch marks and called, strangely, a 'thrower'. (This is the more confusing since the real thrower on the front of the crankshaft is also termed a thrower!) The workshop manual suggests that the cover thrower should be discarded and replaced when a new seal is fitted. Clearly it is possible to damage the thrower if it is simply driven or pressed out.

I decided to try to get the thrower out undamaged. This, in fact, proved to be quite easy. Initially I dug the end of the seal (at the top) out, and once I'd an end about $\frac{1}{2}$ in. long I was able to pull the rest of it out. The next move was to turn the cover onto its face, and using a hammer and a small diamond point chisel, to pare away the 'staking' of the cover where it overlapped the seal.

Next, the end of a broad tyre lever was put into the space where the seal had been, and applying a *little* force at various points around its circumference, the thrower was eased out. The new seal was in the form of a straight strip. This was coiled into the thrower, manipulating it with my fingers so that it all went in *without any trimming to length*. This is vital to get a good seal. The thrower and seal were gently drifted home with the joint in the seal uppermost, until the thrower bottomed in the case. It was then re-staked by deforming the cover, locally, with a centre punch at three points at intervals of about 120 degrees. Following the technique adopted for the rear main seal, the timing cover seal was rubbed down with a hammer shaft until the front pulley would *just* pass through it.

With the oilseal job behind me I returned to the pump. Although lightly scored the gears still had a sufficient 'stand proud' above their casing (see picture) at about 0.0025 in. The casing too was lightly but not excessively scored, so the parts were deemed serviceable and put back together. The entire internal part of the pump was tightly packed with petroleum jelly to ensure its priming at the initial start up. Be certain to do this thoroughly, as priming of the oil pump can be a source of difficulty on these engines.

The relief and by-pass valves in the pump cover were cleaned inspected for damaged faces and finding none, replaced. A snag occurred when I tried to remove the little gauze filter in the relief valve return oil way. It is staked in and in trying to lever it out I broke through the gauze so that the whole thing had to come out to be repaired by soldering before being replaced and restaked to secure it.

Putting the timing cover back on the engine I made sure the jointing faces were clean, especially on the raised high pressure areas surrounding the oil passages and around the

The seal is retained by an aluminium ring, called confusingly a 'thrower'. It is staked in position. Here the staking is being pared away with a diamond point chisel so that the thrower can be levered out

The seal which came in a straight strip has been coiled into the thrower. After refitting the seal with its joint at the top the thrower was re-staked in the cover

waterways between the cylinder block and the timing cover. I made certain that the inlet port was filled with oil to assist in priming.

Although it made the assembly a bit heavy and awkward to handle, I put the cover on with the front pulley inserted through it, turning the pulley to locate it on to its key in the crankshaft as it went home. This avoided the possibility of damaging the graphited seal by pushing a misaligned pulley through it. With the cover bolted into position, (some of the bolts passing through the water pump,) the crankshaft dog screw was tightened to 140 lb. ft. The distributor was temporarily fitted with its rotor arm pointing to no. 1 plug lead segment in the cap whilst no. 1 piston of the engine was at TDC. The object of this was to ensure that the oil pump shaft, which is driven by a blade on the bottom of the distributor shaft, was in the correct position to accept it. Adjustment of the pump shaft was made through the distributor hole in the cover using a long screwdriver. At this stage the distributor could have been left in place and accurately timed, however, having set the oil pump shaft I preferred to leave it out to improve access to the intake manifold gasket-cum-camshaft cover later. The fuel pump was refitted, ensuring that its arm was loca-

The timing cover seal was rubbed down, in the same way as those for the near main bearing, until the front pulley would just pass through

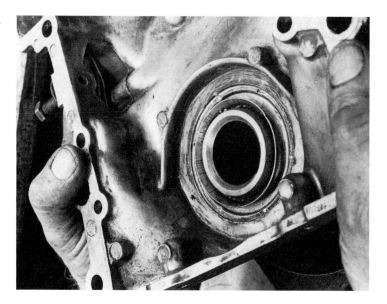

Checking the 'stand proud' of the oil pump gears using a feeler gauge

ted on to its driving eccentric, waggling the body as it was pushed home whilst listening for the characteristic pumping sound. Assured that all was well, the pump was tightened into place. The sump could now be fitted permanently with its new gasket applying gasket cement at its junctions with the timing cover gasket at the front and the side seals for the rear main bearing cap. To complete the work in this area the new oil filter canister was spun on to its thread and lightly tightened by hand.

Cylinder heads and manifolds
Preparing to fit the heads, it was necessary to check that all of the previously cleaned joint faces were still clean and hadn't been accidentally scored as work progressed. New gaskets were fitted ensuring that the 'top' marking was upward, and after giving a squirt of oil to all of the cylinder bores (except 1 and 6 which had their pistons at TDC). The heads were identified as right and left and were located over their dowels. The bolts were cleaned and lubricated before fitting, the three longest going into the centre of the head within the rocker cover and the four shortest going along the outside extremity of the head, leaving seven bolts to go into the remaining holes. The heads were torqued down progressively in the rather unusual recommended sequence (see diagram) through 50 and 60 lb. ft to a final value of 70 lb. ft.

LH head shown

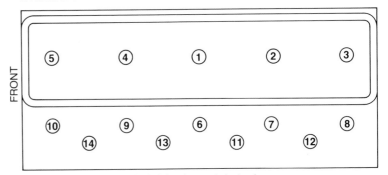

Rover V8 cylinder head bolt tightening and slackening sequence.
Torque 65-70 lb ft.
Long bolts 1 2 4, Medium bolts 3 5 6 7 8 9 10, Short bolts 11 12 13 14

Above: **On re-assembly the oil pump was fully packed with 'Vaseline' petroleum jelly to assist in its initial priming**

Right: **Before the timing cover was refitted the oil thrower (the real thrower) was positioned over its key. The gasket was treated locally with Blue Hylomar where oil and water flow through it**

There's a 'nick' on the end of each rocker shaft. It goes upwards, inwards and to the front for the right-hand shaft, and upwards, outwards and to the rear for that on the left. I had greased the bore of the rockers lightly on assembly and pumped some oil down the oil feed drilling in the cylinder head before fitting the rocker gear. It was necessary to take a little care to get the holes in the rocker pedestals aligned with those in the shaft and to ensure that the long securing bolts screwed into the head by hand. A

Rocker shaft markings; old (left) and new. These marks should be upwards, onwards and to the front for the offside (r) rocker shaft and upwards outwards and to the back for the nearside one

baffle plate is fitted over the front left-hand rockers, and the rear ones on the right.

As the rocker shafts were installed the push rods had to be guided into place. When the engine was dismantled it was very oily externally. A major cause of this was leakage from the rocker covers, the gaskets of which were completely out of position. To avoid a repetition of this, the joint faces in the covers were cleaned, thoroughly allowed to dry and then new gaskets were cemented into place, making sure that the gaskets were the right way round before bringing the glued faces together. The rocker covers were fitted after pouring some engine oil over the assembled rocker gear.

Fitting the intake manifold called for some care since three fluids are separated by it: oil, water and fuel/air mixture. Accordingly the neoprene seals were lubricated with a silicon grease on both sides and located in position, their ends engaging with notches formed between the cylinder heads and the block and their flanges going over the edge of the camshaft/pushrod chest. Hylomar SQ32M sealant was applied to the cylinder head jointing face both sides of the gasket and the ends of the manifold around the waterways. The large sheet metal gasket was put into place

As the rocker shafts are fitted, baffles have to be fitted over them; to the rear on the offside and the front on the nearside

observing the FRONT marking and the pressed steel gasket clamps were fitted front and rear but their single fixing bolts were *only finger tightened* at this stage.

The manifold was located into position and after cleaning and lubricating, the bolts were fitted and tightened progressively *a little at a time* on alternate sides, working from the centre outwards and stopping when a torque of 31 lb. ft was reached. The clamps could then be tightened to 15 lb. ft and the water hoses reconnected.

Inlet manifold. The seals are put in position locating their ends in notches formed between the cylinder block and heads. The gasket is smeared with Blue Hylomar around its waterways at the ends as are the cylinder heads and the manifold. The gasket is positioned taking note of its 'Front' marking. The manifold is put into place and is progressively torqued to 31 lb. ft (41 NM) and the clamps to 15 lb. ft (20 NM)

The exhaust manifolds do not employ gaskets so it was absolutely essential to see that their joint faces were quite clean. Without the assurance of a gasket being there to provide a seal, I felt very tempted to give the bolts a little extra torque 'just to be sure'. However, mindful of how easy it is to strip threads in aluminium the temptation was resisted, tightening the bolts to the recommended 15 lb. ft.

With the engine proper complete, all that remained now, was to fit the various external items that had been removed earlier: carburettors, alternator, power steering pump, starter motor, ring gear and drive plate, torque converter and bell housing. After replacing the 'points' and setting the dwell to 26–28 degrees on a specialized tester the distributor was timed by the static method (see chapter 3) to 3 degrees BTDC to await fine adjustment using a strobe lamp when the engine was once more installed and running.

Chapter 6 | A straight six twin cam

Jaguar engine. The rotor arm is in this position when the front (No. 6) cylinder is firing, 1 and 6 pistons at tdc

The double overhead camshaft engine with semi-hemispherical combustion chambers originated in the first decade of this century and over the years has come to be recognized as the classic format for racing and high performance engines.
Our example
Jaguar adopted the twin cam layout in 1948 and all of their six-cylinder engines of the classic period are developments of that engine. It is sometimes thought that the overhaul of a Jaguar engine is too difficult for the home restorer. It isn't, perhaps, a good engine for the raw beginner to 'cut his teeth' on, but with one or two engine restorations under his belt it should be a reasonable proposition for an intelligent and careful amateur.

In this chapter it is not my intention to write a full case history as I've done in the two preceding chapters. Rather, bearing in mind the sort of restorer this is likely to interest, I will concentrate on the aspects in which the Jaguar twin cam engine differs from those with push rod valve operation.

Cylinder head removal

Although not strictly essential, it is not a bad idea when you are going to take the head off a Jaguar engine to set nos. 1 and 6 pistons at TDC. Start dismantling at the back of the engine by taking the oil feeds off, one for each camshaft. The cambox covers come off next. With these removed, look at the camshaft sprockets, they are retained by two screws. Turn the engine to make the *inaccessible* screws accessible and remove them, re-position the engine to 'TDC 1 & 6'. Remove the breather cover, held by four

Cylinder head showing (right)
camshaft sprocket, one of its
securing screws, wire locking,
adjustment plate and circlip and
(left) the upper chain tensioner
(see text)

When the camshaft bolts are
undone and the chain slackened
the camshaft sprockets are slid
inwards and upwards on to their
support brackets and wired
together to keep them there. The
head can be unbolted and
removed. (Head shown removed
for clarity)

domed nuts. This will expose the upper timing chain tensioner which can be released by slackening the nut, pressing in the little spring loaded plunger and turning the
serrated plate clockwise.

The next step is to return to the camboxes and remove
the two remaining screws from the chainwheels (one in
each), after which the wheels can be slid inwards and
upwards on to their support brackets. *Do not turn the engine
in this condition* or the pistons will foul the valves causing
damage. The 14 head nuts and the six smaller ones securing the timing cover to the head can be undone progressively in the order shown. The head can now be lifted clear.
The valves protrude below the head jointing face so *the
head must not be placed face down on a bench* unless it is
supported at its ends on two blocks of wood of say, $\frac{3}{4}$ in.
square cross section.

Removing the timing gear

With the head out of the way, you can turn your attention
to taking off the sump, it's fairly straightforward. After
releasing the flexible oil pipe from the filter you'll have 26
set screws to remove between the sump and the crankcase
and four nuts between the sump and the timing cover! The
short screw goes to the front on the right.

The front pulley and crankshaft damper has to be taken

Jaguar valves protrude below the head!

Do not **put the cylinder head face down on a bench without a narrow supporting block at the rear (and at the front if the studs have been taken out) or valve damage is likely to occur**

Front pulley assembly L to R cone, pulley/damper plain washer, screw and lockplate

off next. The lockplate has to be removed and the large nut undone. It is then necessary to lever the pulley forward and with the pressure applied give the end of its central cone a sharp blow to release the pulley from the taper on the cone.

Unbolt and remove the water pump and the remaining screws holding the timing cover and ease it off its dowels. Now, at last the 'dog can see the rabbit'. Release and remove the hydraulic tensioner for the lower chain and the two 'damper' pads and undo the four set screws holding the front bracket to the cylinder block. The timing gear assembly can now be lifted clear for attention on the bench.

Timing gear assembly: upper
and lower chains intermediate
and lower vibration damper 1
and 2 and hydraulic chain
tensioner (3). On early engine
turn release screw clockwise to
retract tensioner. On later
engines guard for its extension on
dismantling

1. Dismantling

The assembly can be broken down by removing the nut
and serrated washer from the idler shaft and then taking
out the little locking plunger and spring. Removing four
nuts will allow you to separate the front and back brackets.
Collect the upper chain and idler, dampers for the upper
chain, distance pieces and the top chain retainer as you part

Timing chains can stretch considerably:

a The longer, top, chain is being tested by 'shuffling'

b Testing a chain for wear by 'bowing'

the brackets. Lift the lower chain from the large intermediate wheel. Take the circlip off the end of the shaft carrying the dual intermediate chainwheel and press or gently lever it out of its bracket. The chainwheel can now be removed.

2. Inspection and overhaul

There is, in total, a very long chain run from the crankshaft to the camshafts in the Jaguar engine. The cumulative wear in such a length can be enormous, but the engine is a sophisticated one and provision is made to contend with wear, in the form of an automatic adjuster for the lower chain and a manual adjuster for the top one. The effect of wear on the valve timing can be countered by adjusting the camshaft positions by means of the finely serrated plates on which the sprockets are mounted. Notwithstanding all that has been said it would still be unwise, given the opportunity, not to replace worn chains and their wheels. If a chain can be 'bowed' to any extent, or if it can be 'shuffled' then change it. Chains aren't terribly expensive. You should also examine the chainwheels and

a

Intermediate chain wheel assembly:

a The shaft for the intermediate wheel is passed through it with the larger (28T) sprocket outwards

b The shaft with the wheel on it is pressed (or gently tapped using a soft drift) into its rear support bracket. The roll pin has to be vertical to engage a short slot in the bracket. (Wheel left off for clarity)

c When the shaft is home it is secured by a circlip

b

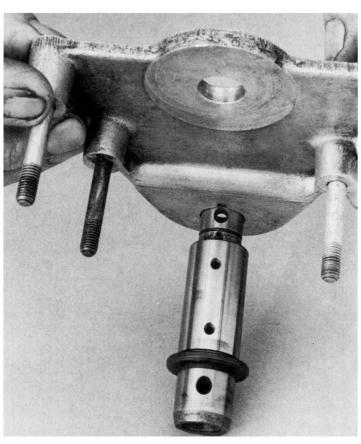

c

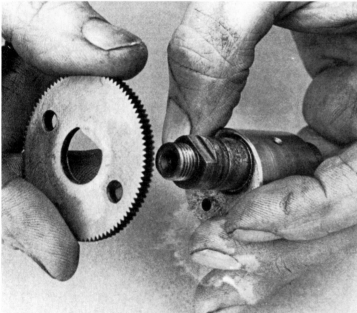

Idler shaft assembly

a The eccentric shaft is pushed through the hole in the front bracket

b The locking plunger and spring are fitted

c They are followed by the eccentric plate, fitting its D shaped hole on to the eccentric shaft

d All is secured by a nut and washer.

(Inset) See that the locating plunger engages the locking plate properly when released

a

Building up the timing gear assembly:

a Assemble the shorter chain on to the larger (28T) sprocket and the longer chain on to the smaller (20T) sprocket. Position the longer upper chain as shown with the bore of the idler sprocket eccentric to the upper hole in the rear plate so as to accept the eccentric shaft

b Carefully bring the brackets together inserting the pegs on the camshaft wheels into the support brackets fitting the upper chain vibration dampers, distance pieces and upper chain retainer. Bolt the assembly together with 4 nuts

c Detail of camshaft sprocket assembly. A 'half tooth' adjustment is possible by turning the serrated plate 180 degrees approximately

b

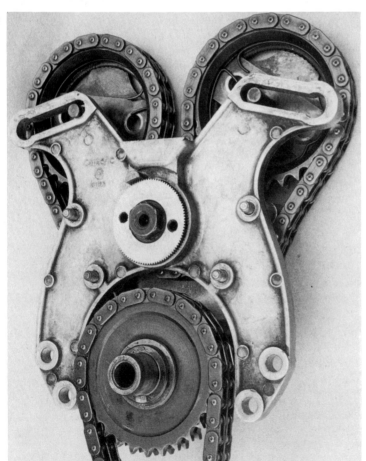

c

the shaft on which the intermediate dual chainwheel runs and in addition the hydraulic tensioner for the lower chain and the sundry dampers.

Reassembly of the timing gear

First, the eccentric shaft for the top chain adjuster is fitted to the front mounting bracket, followed by the locking plunger, its spring, the serrated plate and its nut and shake-proof washer. The idler sprocket is fitted to the eccentric shaft. The dual intermediate sprocket is fitted to its shaft with the larger wheel forward and the shaft is pressed into the lower hole in the middle of the rear bracket and secured by a circlip. Fit the longer top chain to the smaller wheel of the dual intermediate sprocket and the shorter bottom chain to the larger wheel. Thread the longer (top) chain under the idler wheel and assemble the front and rear brackets together securing them with four nuts.

Refitting the timing gear to the engine

If this work is part of a major overhaul you may find it easier to assemble the timing gear with the engine upside-down on the bench. Place the upper chain retainer in front of the front bracket and the two upper chain damper plates and their distance pieces behind the front bracket. Place the four attachment screws in position with shakeproof washers under their heads. Position the lower chain on to the crankshaft sprocket and locate and fit the timing gear to the cylinder block with the four attachment screws. The camshaft sprockets can now, be engaged with the top chain and be placed on their support brackets.

The next job is to fit the hydraulic chain tensioner adjusting the shims behind it, if any, to bring its pad into a centralized position on the lower chain. (Don't forget to clean and refit the little gauze filter in the oil supply line to the tensioner.)

With the pad of the hydraulic tensioner extended about 0.125 in. (3 mm) from its fully retracted position, adjust the intermediate damper plate to touch the chain and then adjust the lower damper to make light contact with the chain.

Refitting the timing cover, water pump and sump is a

Fitting the timing gear:
First *turn the cylinder block over* so that its head face rests on the wooden bench top or blocks of wood. Hang the lower chain over the crankshaft sprocket and using four bolts with shakeproof washers, bolt the assembly to the cylinder block ensuring that the bolts pass through the upper chain retainer, upper chain vibration dampers and distance pieces

reversal of the dismantling procedure, remembering to fit the short sump screw at the front on the right-hand side.

Decarbonizing, grinding valves, valve clearance adjustment

In removing the valves, refitting them, working on the camshafts and around the cylinder head generally, there are a number of points which have to be watched carefully or serious damage may result: The first of these warnings

Later type hydraulic chain tensioner. See text for details of adjustment and the setting of the intermediate and lower chain vibration dampers

Inverted bucket tappet and distance pad for adjustment purposes

has already been given, about the protrusion of the valves below the head. There is, of course, no problem if the camshafts are removed.

Secondly, *do not turn the camshafts when they are disconnected from their drives, or the valves will foul each other.*

The third point is to remind readers that like the Sunbeam and Rover engines, the Jaguar has an aluminium cylinder head and consequently all of the normal precautions and weaknesses pertinent to those apply. Jaguar recommend that steel scrapers are not used when decarbonizing rather that 'worn emery cloth and paraffin' are used to clean and polish the combustion chambers and the valve ports.

The last warning is that it is imperative that all valve train components are kept in their correct sequence, remembering that Jaguar engines number from the flywheel end, i.e. the back piston is no 1.

Frankly, when decoking, I'd depart a little from the maker's 'words of wisdom' and use 320 and 360 'wet and dry' paper rather than worn emery with the paraffin. On these engines the ports and combustion spaces were highly polished. There is some satisfaction to be had in restoring them to that state. Jaguar engines are capable of running for very long periods between overhauls. Quite 'tight' limits are set, for example, for valve to guide clearance;

Checking valve clearance on the back of the cam

With 6 and 1 (front and rear) pistons at top dead centre and the front (6) cylinder firing as indicated by the rotor arm (photo page 91), use the Jaguar timing gauge to position the camshaft. (This particular gauge was made by the owner of the engine)

so that you might find that you have to scrap a good-looking valve because it's got a little over 0.003 in. wear on its stem. Don't be tempted to 'let it go' in the interest of economy. The secret of those long intervals between top overhauls is making sure that it starts off right.

Valve removal on Jaguar engines entails screwing a wooden block shaped to fit inside the combustion chamber, to the workbench or to a substantial board. The head is placed over this and the valve springs pushed down to release the collets. There is a factory approved tool, but take a look at a 'home-made' tool illustrated in chapter 1 in use on the head of a six-cylinder Alfa having a very similar layout to the Jaguar engine.

Whilst it's unlikely, if you need guides for your valves or those 'inverted bucket' tappets, you'll need a well-equipped machine shop to put them in for you. Incidentally, with reference to machine shops, Jaguar only advise reboring cylinders up to 0.030 in. after which the dry cylinder liners may be pressed out and replaced.

Valve grinding is done in the usual way, after, if necessary, light refacing of the valve seatings and those in the head. You'll need your local friendly machine shop for this.

With the valves refitted you'll need to set the valve clearances. To risk stating the obvious; there is no room for error when carrying out this operation on a Jaguar engine. If you discover on starting your engine that you've got 'em wrong, there is nothing for it except to take it all down again to put things right. Remember too, that if there has to be an error, it makes sense to err on the 'big' side. A wide clearance will cause some noise, but a 'tight' one will almost certainly lead to a burnt valve and perhaps burning of the seat in the cylinder head. Certainly, such damage would necessitate a premature top overhaul.

When you've ground in the valves and refitted them, fit one camshaft to its correct side with the tappets and pads in position. The tappets must be in good shape with no indentation or pitting where they contact the cams and their diametral clearance in their guides must lie between 0.008 in. and 0.002 in. The shaft is turned so that each tappet, in turn, rests on the back of its cam and the valve clearance is checked between the tappet and the cam measuring it with a feeler gauge. As you measure each clearance, record it. Take out the tappets one by one and record the letter on each pad, or if it is indistinct, measure its thickness using a micrometer or a vernier gauge. (You might find a suction type valve grinding stick useful in lifting out the tappets.)

The adjusting pads are sized from 0.085 in. to 0.110 in. in steps of 0.001 in. denoted by letters A-Z, so suppose you discover your inlet valves have a 0.07 in clearance where it should be 0.004 in. and the pad is lettered 'B' (0.086), you'll need an 'E' pad (0.089 in.) to correct it. Remember, too, that the letter (or thickness) is not the only criterion by which a pad is retained or rejected. If there is any indentation where it contacts its valve, then it must be discarded. Having selected your pads refit them and the tappets followed by the camshaft and physically check with the feeler gauge that you 'got your sums right'. Remove the camshaft and repeat the checking and setting operations for the other side.

Fitting the cylinder head and valve timing

As the camshafts are finally fitted after adjusting the valve clearances set their positions with their key ways perpendicular to the cam box. To do this accurately you'll need

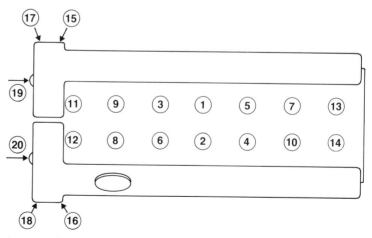

Jaguar 4.2 E type engine. Sequence for cylinder head nut tightening and slackening. Nuts 15-18 screw on to studs fitted on the lower face of the head. With 19 and 20, these are 5/16 in. dia.

Removing plug from a Jaguar crankshaft

the Jaguar timing gauge. Turn the engine to bring the front cylinder (no. 6) to TDC and check, from the position of the rotor arm in the distributor, that no. 6 is in its firing position. Ensure that the jointing faces on the cylinder head and block are clean and free of grease. An evaporative solvent is recommended by the makers, but these are either highly flammable (petrol, thinners) or they give off toxic fumes (carbon tetrachloride). I'd use methylated spirit. Whatever you do be careful! Fit a new gasket, observing the 'top' marking. Place the head in position and torque it down to 58 lb ft in the sequence shown. The valve timing can now be set. It is impractical on these engines to mark the timing in the common way partly because the relative inaccessibility of the timing gear would render any checking difficult and partly because the speed reduction between the crankshaft and the camshaft is in two stages with the dual intermediate chainwheel running at $\frac{3}{4}$ crankshaft speed and the camshaft's running at $\frac{2}{3}$ of the speed of the intermediate chainwheel. The first thing is to see that no. 6 (front) piston is exactly at TDC. Move the camshaft sprockets from their support brackets and place them over the flanges on the shafts and tension the top timing

The build-up of sludge which was revealed

chain by releasing its locking nut, through the breather aperture at the front of the head, pushing in the spring loaded plunger and turning the serrated plate anti-clockwise. Release the plunger and tighten the nut. *The chain must not be dead tight.* Next, tap the sprockets off their flanges and take out the large circlips so that you can detach the serrated adjusting plates. Ensure by checking with the gauge that the camshafts are *exactly* in position and if not, correct them. Replace the sprockets on to the camshaft flanges and position the serrrated plate so that the two bolt holes are aligned and secure it by its circlip. It is *essential* that the holes are exactly aligned or the timing will be incorrect. If the bolts won't start easily, remove the plate and turn it through 180 degrees when, due to the relationship between the positions of the serrations and the holes, it should allow the screws to start easily. With the engine at TDC 1 & 6 you'll only be able to start one screw in each camshaft. Tighten these and turn the engine to gain access to the other two screw holes. With both screws tight, check first the top chain tension, then turn the engine to exactly TDC and check that the camshafts are exactly in position as indicated by the gauge. If all is well, lock the screws on the camshaft sprockets with wire. If not, I'm afraid you'll have to back track to put it right. The rest of the engine assembly is straightforward.

FOOTNOTE:

At any time when you've got the sump off your Jaguar engine it's an excellent idea to remove the plugs blanking off the hollow crankpins and clean the spaces behind them. We took the plugs out of the crankshaft of our Jaguar. The photographs show what we found.

Chapter 7 | Some nasties!

As this book has progressed, various problems have been noted. The sort of things that to the enthusiast may seem insuperable or catastrophic. It may, of course, be that they are insuperable or catastrophic!—but taking a more optimistic view—I'll try in this chapter to look at a few of these problems starting with cylinder heads which are difficult to remove.

One of the most difficult problems one can encounter is the removal of an aluminium alloy cylinder head where an electrolytic action between the studs and the head has produced a brownish white compound between the studs and the head which wedges the studs in their holes so that the head is immovable. Aluminium heads for side-valve engines were in vogue from the mid 1930s continuing in production cars (e.g. the Triumph Mayflower) through to the mid-fifties.

This is a very nasty problem. If you are taking one of these heads off and initially you've no idea of whether the studs are free in their holes, it's a good idea having cleared any impeding fittings out of the way to slacken the head *with the engine cold* in the correct sequence and then screw each nut up on its stud until it is flush. Thoroughly douse each stud hole with Plus Gas A releasing fluid and take yourself off for a coffee, cigarette or whatever for about ten minutes. When you return use a 2 lb (1 kg.) hammer sideways on the nuts to jar the studs; apply more Plus Gas A, as you do so observing whether there seems to be a clearance around the stud or not.

Finally, with the nut flush, give the stud several sharp, firm vertical blows. Treat them all in this way and your tight head may yield. It's very likely that having done all

Lifting handles made of $\frac{1}{2}$ in. bore iron water pipe and old spark plug bodies with long reach plugs are useful in removing tight cylinder heads from side valve engines

that the head will still be resolutely stuck, you'll be feeling frustrated and impotent, imagining the inanimate head to be quietly smirking and mocking you. A very useful diversion at this stage would be to make up two lifting handles (three for a six-cylinder) to assist in the removal of the head. Each of these consists of the body of a 14 mm *long reach* spark plug welded to a piece of $\frac{1}{2}$ in. iron water pipe say 5 in. long topped by another piece say 6 in. long at right angles to it.

The first use of your lifters is to screw them in in place of the sparking plugs and try to rock the head violently sideways, preferably whilst someone tries to tap the studs and apply Plus Gas . . . and if it still doesn't move?

On some heads a lug is provided front and rear which overlaps beyond the block, to which a hammer can be applied, but this may not help much.

Some people might advocate the use of hydraulic force to move the head. The method is as follows:

Turn the engine until the inlet valve on one of the engine cylinders has just closed indicating the beginning of the power stroke. Remove the spark plug and fill the cylinder with a gear oil (SAE 140) replace the plug and using as much force as you can apply, turn the engine in its normal direction of rotation via the dog nut.

This method will often shift a stuck head but:

When experiencing difficulty in deciding where to position the offset drive shaft for the distributor. The position of No. 1 lead can sometimes be determined by first offering the cap up to the head as shown. This 'fixes' the rotor position and that in turn determines the position of the tongue on the distributor shaft and in turn that of the slot in the drive shaft

a Triumph TR5 cylinder block showing disastrous damage after a piston break up

b The same cylinder after re-sleeving and boring back to size

a

b

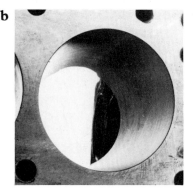

a) as soon as the head moves oil squelches out to make a terrible mess of the engine, car, mechanic, garage and whatever, and

b) having lifted the head perhaps $\frac{1}{16}$ in., it's still tight on the studs. So on balance I wouldn't do this.

I'd try using some shock loading to move it, supplemented with the weight of the car.

The two or three lifters are screwed into the head so that their top tubes are in line and with the head nuts still flush or just below flush. A piece of half inch silver steel bar is 'threaded' through the top tube of the lifters. The crane is now attached to this bar and the engine lifted until the sump is on the point of leaving the bench (or the front wheels of the car are on the point of leaving the ground!) A slide hammer with an adaptor to fit the head studs is screwed on to each in turn and hammered downwards with some determination preferably after an overnight soaking with the engine suspended . . . and if it still doesn't move?

Well, . . . there used to be some special cutters made of tubular tool steel which passed over the stud and enlarged the hole, cutting out the corrosion as they went. An excellent idea, but these sometimes got bent due to hammering or lost their cut. I'd buy a set today if I could get them.

If your head is still immovable and the engine is on the

Badly seated big end shells suggesting mismatched caps. (Sunbeam)

bench some gentle all-over heat preferably from a large blow lamp might help, although you'd have to get the head face subsequently trued. This might be just about all you could do without resorting to the tactic I once had to use on a Humber Hawk, that of taking off the sump, removing the two middle connecting rods and pistons and driving the head off with a 4 lb hammer and a block of oak passed through the cylinders! As an aside, one mechanic I used to know used vinegar rather than Plus Gas or a penetrating oil as a releasing agent for aluminium heads. There could be 'some mileage' in this idea.

A problem with a 'basket case' engine is sometimes that there is an offset tongue distributor drive but the rebuilder doesn't know the position of this relative to the engine. Providing that the distributor, its cap, rotor arm and leads are available, sort it out like this:

1) offer the distributor loosely into place and determine from the length and position no. 1 (front) lead, note its position in the cap;

2) determine by turning the engine and watching the sequence of *either* the inlet *or* the exhaust valves, the firing order (for a four-cylinder it will most likely be 1342);

3) knowing this, if the leads are marked you can determine the direction of distributor rotation, if not look for a marking on the unit, or perhaps an arrow on the rotor arm. If this fails you'll have to do it by temporarily inserting the drive and turning the engine;

4) set the distributor so that the rotor is pointing towards the cap electrode for no. 1 cylinder and *turning in the correct direction of rotation* so that the contacts are just separating. *Note the position of the offset tongue on the distributor shaft*;

5) turn the engine in the direction of rotation; watch the inlet valve push rod rise and fall indicating the beginning of the compression stroke;

6) move the engine on until the piston is say, $\frac{1}{16}$ in. (1.8 mm) before TDC;

7) insert the drive shaft so that the slot in the drive is in the correct position to engage the tongue of the distributor in the previously established position without turning when the drive shaft is right home.

'Lost' valve timing may seem even more worrying than

Above and above centre: **Side view of caps supporting mismatched suggestion**

Above right: **Cap in correct position.**
Note: machining marks now match in contrast to previous illustration

lost ignition timing. Let's consider this problem two ways:

1) There are no marks but you have some data, say inlet valve opens 12 degrees BTDC. The drill here is first of all to find TDC as accurately as possible. Turn the engine until the piston is at some specific point from the top edge of the cylinder, say 1 cm. Mark the flywheel opposite a specific datum point on the crankcase backplate or bell housing. Now turn the engine *backwards* until the piston is again 1 cm from the top of the cylinder and mark the flywheel again. Find the mid-point between your marks and make a third mark. Move that mark to a point opposite your datum and you have TDC accurately. With that done count the teeth on the flywheel, say there are 120, then each tooth represents $\frac{360°}{120} = 3°$, so the inlet valve should open '4 teeth' before TDC.

Set the piston on no. 1 cylinder to 4 teeth before TDC (turning in the direction of rotation). Turn the camshaft, fitted in the block with the tappets for no. 1 cylinder in place, and determine as accurately as you can the point at which the inlet tappet begins to lift. At this juncture connect the crankshaft to the camshaft by fitting the timing chain or if necessary, the chain and sprockets as an assembly. Check as follows:

Assemble the no. 1 inlet valve to the cylinder head. Fit the head temporarily followed by the push rod for no. 1 inlet valve and the rocker shaft. Set the valve to its normal clearance on the back of the cam. Turn the engine slowly in its normal direction of rotation, at the same time twisting the push rod between your fingers. When the rod just becomes too tight to turn the engine should be at 12 degrees or four teeth before TDC. If this is not so you

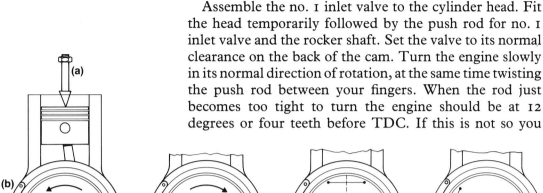

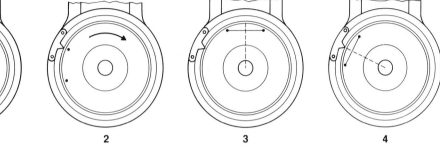

1 Fix a stop (a) to a cylinder head stud with a nut and distance piece. Attach a pointer (b) at any point around the circumference of the flywheel with *two* or more bolts. Turn the engine gently until it is stopped by the piston touching the pointer. Make a dot mark at the periphery of the fly wheel

2 Turn the engine gently in the opposite direction until the piston is stopped again. Mark this point as before

3 Draw a line between the two dots, find its centre by measuring or bisecting, and draw a new line at 90 degrees to the first (it should, if projected, pass through the centre of the flywheel)

4 Position the radial line opposite your pointer, and the piston is at TDC

Finding TDC diagram

may need to move the camshaft sprocket 'one tooth' one way or the other. Once you are satisfied on this score the temporarily fitted head can be removed and assembly resumed in the ordinary way.

Supposing you have no data at all to work with, what then? It is a reasonable assumption that the 'overlap' of the valves is about equal; that is to say that the number of degrees by which the inlet valve opens before TDC is approximately the same as the number of degrees by which the exhaust closes after TDC. With this in mind, if we set 1 and 4 pistons at TDC (or 1 and 6 for a six-cylinder) with the cams for no. 1 cylinder pointing 'equally downwards' and those for no. 4 (or 6) 'equally upwards' as in our diagram and then connect the drive, the engine is likely to run satisfactorily.

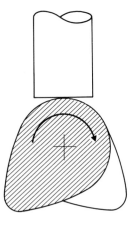

CAMS EQUALLY DOWN

The position the camshaft should be in when no. 1 piston is at TDC firing. Exhaust cam nearer

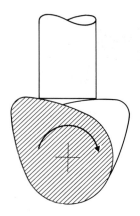

CAMS EQUALLY UP

The position the camshaft should be showing the cams for no. 4 (or no. 6) cylinder when no. 1 is firing. Inlet cam nearer

When a major breakup occurs within an engine it is often automatically concluded that the entire engine is scrap. Pause for a moment to allow your anger, embarrassment or self recrimination to subside. Take some time to weigh up the possibilities of reclamation.

One such problem is that where a piston breaks up and the broken eye of the little end of the connecting rod goes through the cylinder wall into the water jacket. On occasions a specialist repair has been possible by having the block bored out to take a thick cylinder liner which is then pushed in, at a substantial interference over the damage and bored back to size. Some accompanying photographs depict a Triumph TR5/six-cylinder block before and after such a repair. Such a course of action is likely to be cheaper and better than buying an 'unknown' engine from the scrap yard.

A difficulty with which the engine repairer is, sometimes, beset is that of accidentally transposed big end caps. On the Sunbeam engine, featured in chapter 4, I had this problem to contend with. Before any rebuilding work could begin the suspected mismatch of the connecting rods and their caps had to be investigated. I viewed this prospect with some apprehension. As will be seen from the photographs the big end shells were showing uneven wear patterns indicative of this sort of fault. What could be established? The rods were clearly 'dot' marked so there was no question about their sequence, there were oil holes to direct oil to the thrust side (i.e. the 'off' side) of the cylinder walls so it was easy to check that the connecting rods were the right way round. Finally the locating lugs for the shell bearings were both on the same side of the connecting rod, but at opposite ends of the bearing, indicating that the caps were the right way round.

The only remaining error there could be was that the caps were not in their correct order from front to rear. I was, it seemed, offered two possible lines of action. Either using new bearings, to try and sort it out by trial and error, or to get down to some careful measurement. The second seemed to be the more logical way, but I couldn't because of their small diameter, use an internal micrometer to measure the bore of the big end eyes, so perhaps I should

resort to using a telescopic gauge and an outside micrometer. Now the telescopic gauge can be a bit tedious to use and in transferring the measurement to the micrometer there is a risk of error, so my logical approach began to look as though it would consume a lot of time and still, perhaps not be as accurate as I would like. I mused about a visual/tactile examination and idly fingering the parts my thumb 'suggested', on no. 2 rod, a small discrepancy in the alignment of cap and the rod radially; i.e. the two half circles were out of line.

Secondly, bright areas at one side of the shell in the cap and the opposite side of that in the rod suggested misalignment. I wondered if the caps for 2 and 3 rods had been interchanged; misalignment of the roughly ground flats running the length of the bolt holes suggested that this was more than likely. By switching the caps around a perfect match was achieved. Turning the rod through 90 degrees, a look at the machining marks revealed a perfect match.

With nos. 2 and 3 sorted out it seemed probable that 1 and 4 had been accidentally switched in the same way. At this stage I fitted the new bearings and reassembled each rod in turn to its crankpin and checked that everything now was perfectly free and revolving easily. Clearly what had happened was that at a previous overhaul the caps had been laid out in order but there had been an error made as to which was 1 and which was 4, so that no. 1 cap was fitted to no. 4, no. 2 to no. 3, no. 3 to no. 2 and no. 4 to no. 1. The engine now turned freely. This, I should add, is a fairly unusual technical conundrum, but faced with one of these, stop, summon up all the native wit and reasoning you possess and using your eyes and fingers try to sort it out in the way I have described.

(Above) **Same cap in correct position**

(Top) **End view of transposed cap**

Chapter 8 | Engine cooling systems

This chapter's title says it's about cooling systems but if I were going to be pedantic I'd say we should be considering the engine temperature control system. Many motorists fail to appreciate the need to maintain a certain minimum temperature, although everyone seems to have an intuitive regard for the effects of overheating.

If the engine runs at a low temperature there is likely to be condensation of some of the products of the combustion process, these may have a corrosive acid content. The liquid condensate then finds its way into the crankcase to amalgamate with lubricating oil to produce a repulsive looking sludge which will seriously impede the flow of engine oil due to the restriction of the oil ways and spoil the oil's performance as a lubricant (see chapter 5!)

A too low temperature also has a direct adverse effect on power output and fuel economy because a good deal of the heat which should be usefully employed will be flowing to the water.

Finally, if the engine is seriously over-cooled, unvapourized petrol may also settle on the cylinder walls to dilute the oil with potentially dire results.

The cooling system can be broken down into the following units:

Radiators
Pressure caps
Hoses
Heater unit and hoses
Thermostats
Water pumps
Engine water jackets

We might also wish to consider anti-freeze mixtures and cooling system inhibitors.

A cooling problem capable of diy solution. The airways of this Mini radiator are choked 'solid' with road dirt that has accumulated on leaked engine oil. See text for cleaning method

This chapter will review these items from a practical restoration point of view with the exception of engine water jackets which have been dealt with in chapter 2.

Radiators

These are relatively trouble free. On cars that have stood for many years the radiator might be 'furred up' like a kettle and be totally resistant to de-scaling. Although, in my youth I once took a radiator to pieces, cleaned it and put it back together, I'm not going to recommend it. If you are really satisfied that your radiator is clogged, then buy another or get a specialist to deal with yours.

There have been numerous rigs devised, over the years, to test waterflow through radiators, but in practice, rule of thumb tests are generally adequate. If, using a wide necked water can as used on garage forecourts, or a bucket and a funnel with a large (say $1\frac{1}{2}$ in.) pipe, you 'jerk' a couple of gallons of water into the 'rad' top tank with the bottom hose removed, it should all run through almost instantly. Any significant hesitation to do so says 'fit a new unit'.

One radiator failing especially common on some transverse engined cars, is that leaked lubricating oil finds its way on to the radiator matrix where road dirt, dead insects and God knows what, adheres to it. If the airways are blocked the engine will overheat just as effectively as though the blockage were in the water pipes. Fortunately, something can be done about this fault by washing off the oil and assorted 'gubbins' using first, some paraffin and an old paint brush, being careful to brush gently. This can be followed by a solution of hot water and detergent. If you're one of those well-equipped types who has a compressor at his disposal, dry the matrix and clear the airways finally by this means.

Radiator pressure caps

The radiator pressure cap has since the early postwar years played an essential role in the operation of the cooling system. By pressurizing the system, the boiling point of the water is raised. This can have the beneficial effect of allowing the engine to run at a higher temperature, yield-

Radiator pressure cap

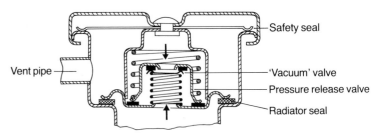

ing improvements in both economy and power and reducing radiator dimensions and the quantity of coolant necessary.

You can visually inspect the seal on the bottom of the radiator cap. If it has deteriorated to any extent, a pressure loss and hence, a water loss will occur, throwing, in all probability nasty red rusty stains all over your pristine engine! Replace it, there's not much else *you* can do about checking the pressure cap. You can take your cap to a garage and get it checked though. They'll have a little pump affair with a pressure gauge. The cap is fitted to it with a suitable adaptor and pumped up until the pressure

A commercial radiator tester in use

valve in the cap 'blows off'. The pressure needed to unseat the valve should, obviously, be the same as that stamped on the cap. The cap should also be able to maintain that pressure without loss.

The instrument used to test the cap is also used to test the system in two ways:

a) The pump, with a suitable adaptor is applied to the radiator in place of the cap and the 'rad' is pressurized to the setting of the cap. When the pumping stops, the pressure should remain constant. If it doesn't a search must be made for a leak (including the car interior in case the heater is leaking.) If nothing is revealed and yet the pressure falls the leak must be into the engine—most likely across the cylinder head gasket into a combustion chamber. Supporting evidence would be an oily scum floating on the water in the radiator top tank and/or signs of an excessive discharge from the filler neck vent pipe.

b) To confirm such a diagnosis, the pressure is released and the tester refitted. The engine is started and run, a rapidly rising pressure indicating that pressure is now finding its way from the combustion chambers into the radiator. To get this confirmation it is sometimes necessary to load the engine for a few seconds, on an automatic transmission vehicle by putting it into 'drive' and holding it on the brakes. For a manual gearbox vehicle the harsher method of slipping the clutch whilst holding the foot brake on with the car in gear has to be adopted. If your suspicions are confirmed the cause may be no more sinister than a cylinder head gasket but if your car's got an aluminium head it could, sadly, be suffering in the way of the one pictured in chapter 4, from corrosion. Repairable but likely to be costly.

Radiator hoses

Synthetic rubber hoses sometimes harden to the extent that their flexibility is lost and engine vibration can crack the metal pipes at the radiator top and bottom tanks. To avoid these problems it's a good idea to fit new hoses every two years if you can get them. If you are taking a radiator out or working on the engine and suspect that the hoses have hardened it's better to saw through them rather than damage a fragile radiator by twisting them off.

A way of ridding a heater of an
air lock. When a steady stream of
water, free of air, issues from the
heater return pipe, it is fitted
quickly, preferably with the
engine running at a fast idle
(1000–2000 rev/min) (Morris 1000
engine)

Heaters and hoses

The matrix of a heater is of similar construction to that
of the radiator but it is, of course, smaller. In looking for
the causes of poor heater performance in a complete
assembled vehicle, it is sensible to ensure that the system
is operating at the correct temperature, (see section on
thermostats) that the fan belt is properly tensioned, so that
the water pump is positively driven, that the heater hoses
are not restricted by deposits from the coolant or by kink-
ing and that the heater system is free of air locks. To satisfy
yourself on this last point it may be necessary to bleed the
heater. Unlike domestic heating systems bleeding arrangements are not generally provided on cars. My method is
to disconnect the return hose from the heater, which usually goes to the water pump, at the water pump end, and
to run the engine at a brisk speed—say 2000 rev/min. with
the disconnected end held over a bucket until a full bore
flow of water is obtained. If it is safe to do so, the pipe
should be pushed on to its connector with the engine running, but *don't take risks*. If your hands seem uncomfort-
ably near that revolving pulley, belt or whatever they are
almost certainly at risk. Shut the engine down and as you
do so bend the heater return hose into a sharp kink, as near
to the disconnected end as possible, push the hose on to
its connector, start the engine and give it a run *at once* to
clear the little 'slug' of air near the pump. Once satisfied
that the return hose is hot tighten the clip holding the hose.

There has been an enormous variety of linkages, cable
systems, and rod arrangements to control water valves and
to operate flaps to direct air to interiors or to the screen
and to distribute heat, front and rear. All of these are liable
to wear and maladjustment. The great diversity of these
arrangements prevents any very specific advice being
given, but if the performance of the system is below par,
some detective work on your back under the dash is likely
to show what needs to be done.

When a car is undergoing a full restoration, it's a good
idea to take out the heater installation, test the matrix for
leaks or for restriction and to give the motor a 'once over'.
With everything assembled these units can be very difficult
to get at so if you are stripping out a bodyshell do it then

and avoid the hassle later. A companion volume in this series deals with the heater motor.

To conclude on heaters, and mainly for those with concours aspirations; long, sagging underbonnet heater pipes can spoil an otherwise tidy layout. A 'cheaty' solution is to make up replicas of the pipe run you want in copper pipe (from plumber's supplies) of the same, or marginally smaller, outside diameter as the bore of your pipes, leaving the ends about 1 in. (25 mm) short. This done you warm your copper pipe and some black plastic pipe of suitable diameter by immersing it in hot water and keeping the materials as hot as you can bear, gradually force the plastic over the copper. This is a tedious and uncomfortable job but it will ensure a good appearance . . . the heater performance will be a little reduced—but if winning counts. . . .

Thermostats

Up until the 1960s thermostats were of the alcohol bellows type. These consist of a metal bellows, partly filled with an alcohol which boils at a temperature well below the boiling point of water. The air is then excluded so that the bellows is forced into a contracted position by atmospheric pressure. The bellows is supported by a framework which carries a valve, so that as the alcohol is heated its vapour pressure forces the bellows to expand, opening the valve.

To obtain the correct setting the disc valve is soldered on to its shank while the temperature is held at the required opening value. As the bellows cools it tries to contract and thus the valve is held firmly shut below its opening temperature. The principle virtue of this type of thermostat is that if the bellows is punctured, it will expand opening the water valve so that it 'fails safe'. In the short term overcooling is preferable to overheating.

Bellows thermostats have been superseded by wax element types because as we have seen the bellows type relies on vapour pressure for its operation so that they aren't really suitable for use in pressurized cooling systems. The wax element thermostat employs a strong metal capsule which contains a special wax. A pointed thrust pin is inserted into the capsule and the space between the wax

Bellows thermostat. Note that at room temperature the valve is open indicating that the bellows have been punctured

a **Ugh! Wax element thermostat as removed from our Sunbeam engine. The result of standing with no water in the system**

b **Cleaned up. Note opening temperature stamped on base of capsule**

c **Despite its 'ordeal' the thermostat tested perfectly**

a

b

c

and the pin is sealed by a rubber sleeve. The wax used has the characteristic of undergoing a considerable change in volume as it changes its state from a solid to a liquid when it melts as the result of increasing temperature. When this occurs the thrust pin is forced outwards opening the valve. This operation is independent of the pressure in the system, so in this respect the wax element thermostat is to be preferred to the bellows type, however, when a wax thermostat fails it cannot be guaranteed to 'fail safe'.

Testing a thermostat consists of a little more than just dunking it in hot water or pouring hot water over it, if we are to get anything more than a very rough and ready result. We tested the thermostat from the Sunbeam engine featured in chapter 4. Its opening temperature was stamped on the bottom of the wax capsule.

The thermostat and a thermometer having a suitable scale were *suspended* in a heatproof glass container half filled with cool water. Under this a stove was placed and the temperature gradually increased until the valve began to open at 82 degrees. By 90 degrees it was fully open. The heat was turned off at this point to avoid the risk of water boiling over or the breakage of the glass bowl. As the temperature fell it was noted that the valve closed at 76, indicating that it was in a sound condition.

Most thermostats have in their top flange a small vent hole to prevent the trapping of air in the cylinder head when the system is filled. A 'jiggle pin' is placed in the hole does just that, keeping the hole open. A serious steam pocket here could do a lot of damage.

Water pumps

Water pumps use a special long bearing unit which is part of the shaft assembly. Failures are generally of this bearing or of the revolving seal. In principle water pumps are reconditionable. Overhaul kits are often listed. In practice I've found it very difficult to buy a water pump overhaul kit.

There is nothing to be gained by dismantling the water pump if you haven't got the necessary reconditioning parts. Old seals and the bearing unit are likely to give trouble if disturbed.

Reconditioning the pump is a fairly straightforward business but an extractor may be necessary to remove the impeller and the drive flange and a press, whilst not essential, makes reassembly a lot easier. Some measurements are essential before beginning so that things go back in their proper position. These measurements are usually the distance from the back face of the impeller to the end of the spindle, usually flush, and from the rear face of the pump to the front of the driving face for the pulley.

In most cases a locking screw locates the bearing assembly. In the case of the Rover pump there is no such location but the pump body which is of aluminium has to be immersed in boiling water and the bearing unit pressed out and replaced to the correct depth whilst hot.

The procedure to overhaul the Sunbeam water pump is as follows:

The single countersunk screw and nut holding the rear cover plate has to be removed. The impeller can now be pulled from its shaft using a three-jaw puller. After the bearing locating screw (if fitted) is removed the spindle and bearing can be pressed or driven out of the casing and the fan driving flange can be pulled or pressed off the spindle. The rubber seal is pushed backwards out of the housing.

Reassembly begins by pushing the spindle and bearing assembly home pressing on its outer diameter. Once in position the screw is located. The seal is fitted from the rear with the metal support facing forward and the seal itself rearward. The face of the seal is lightly greased, and the pulley flange and impeller are pushed home so that the end of the shaft is flush with the impeller rear face and the distance from the rear face of the pump to the front of the pulley flange is 4.870 in. plus or minus 0.005 in. The rear cover can now be fitted with its countersunk screw and a new gasket.

Fans

You tend to think that there is not much to go wrong with the humble fan. It is, after all, just a twisted blade of metal, however, because of its high rotational speed it is a stressed part and can crack. I once saw a fan blade go through the bonnet of a glossy 1938 Hillman Minx. On inspecting the blade afterwards it was obvious from the rusting at the crack that it had been weakened for a very long time. MORAL: whenever you remove the fan, take a minute or so to inspect it for cracking. Be certain too that on refitting the blades are the right way round. There are instances where they can be reversed, using valuable energy to prevent your engine being cooled!

On the topic of energy conservation, a fan that isn't continuously driven can make a significant contribution to fuel economy and reduce engine noise.

Electric fans

The Kenlowe fan or similar is well known and may be mounted in front of or behind the radiator. When fitted retrospectively in the 'classic' period these fans were generally controlled by a thermostatic switch inserted into the bottom hose. To test the fan; with the ignition on and the engine stopped the switch terminals are bridged and the fan should run. We sometimes used to fit a little shorting switch across these thermostatic switches so that the owner could periodically check the fan. In some installations a warning lamp was wired in parallel with the fan motor so that one could tell from the driver's seat when it was running. Either of these ideas can be easily incorporated.

Another energy-saving arrangement is to have a fan mounted on the waterpump spindle via a bearing which also supports a magnetic armature mounted on spring steel arms. Behind this, keyed to the spindle is the water pump pulley which incorporates an electromagnetic winding. When the temperature is sufficiently high a thermostatic switch, housed in a capsule in the cylinder head closes and feeds current via a stationary carbon brush and a slip ring incorporated into the pulley to the electromagnet which attracts the armature towards it so that the fan is driven. Possible faults here are the thermostatic switch (which can be bridged out for test purposes) and a poor connection as the result of a worn brush or a dirty slip ring.

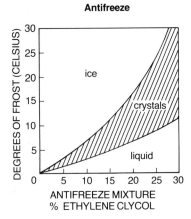

Antifreeze

DEGREES OF FROST (CELSIUS)

ice

crystals

liquid

ANTIFREEZE MIXTURE
% ETHYLENE CLYCOL

Anti-freeze solutions

It makes good sense to keep an anti-freeze solution in your cooling system all the year round, but in order to retain the effectiveness of the corrosion inhibitor which is incorporated in all modern anti-freezes I'd advise flushing out the system and renewing the anti-freeze at the beginning of alternate winters.

If yours is an aluminium alloy engine it's most important to use an anti-freeze solution containing a corrosion inhibitor all year round or if you live in a temperate zone where there are no frosts then a 'straight' inhibitor should be used. Satisfactory anti-freezes are any which conform to British Standard no. BS 3150 or to MIL-E-559 formulation.

A graph shows the relationship between the strength of anti-freeze solutions and the temperatures at which crystallization and solidification occurs. Crystallization will cause no harm to an engine if it isn't run with the coolant in this condition. If it is run the ensuing 'slush' will block the radiator and stop circulation.

Air cooling

Most enthusiasts know that air-cooled engines do not freeze or boil. It is, of course self evident, but nonetheless we were frequently reminded of these facts by VW advertising during the long production life of the Beetle.

What isn't perhaps common knowledge on such a large scale is that two inherent advantages of the air-cooled arrangement are:

1 Because boiling doesn't raise problems, these engines can be run a little hotter, thus reducing the heat loss to coolant, improving the engine's thermal efficiency and yielding a few more miles to the gallon.
2 Because it is not necessary to carry a few gallons of water and a heavy copper radiator around, the power/weight ratio of air-cooled engines is generally better than that for those with liquid cooling.

Set against these advantages the necessary cowling and ducting needed to direct air around the engine can hamper accessibility or allow a dangerous leak to go unnoticed. An

If you've an air cooled engine; this is that of a VW Beetle, fan belt tension is vital. Keep yours tight but not *too* tight and be sure to carry a spare

example of this was the oil cooler used on some VW models. If this leaked it used to spew oil over two near side cylinders. Road dirt and all sorts of airborne rubbish blown by the fan adhered to this 'goo' clogging the spaces between the cooling fins. Before too long, with two cylinders overheating, distorting and perhaps causing local piston seizure the owner was in trouble—be warned.

Be warned too on air-cooled engines, of the possibility of exhaust gas finding its way into the car's interior from the heat exchangers which pick up heat from the outside of the exhaust system for interior heating purposes.

Carbon monoxide is lethal and not always instantly recognized.

Less sinister disadvantages of air-cooled engines are the considerable amount of power needed to drive the cooling fan, the noise that it makes and the fact that the fins on the cylinders and heads can resonate thus amplifying mechanical noises.

Thermostatic control of the coolant (air) on these engines is sometimes managed by a bellows type thermostat, basically the same as that described for liquid-cooled engines but operating a 'throttle ring' through a linkage to restrict the amount of air reaching the cooling fan. The thermostat used here could, like those for liquid-cooled systems, be tested by immersion provided it opened below 100 degrees C. Whenever the opportunity presents itself (as at engine overhauls) the thermostat linkage should be checked for free movement. The fan belt and its tension are vital where the fan is belt driven; be certain that your belt is tight, that you carry a spare and you know how to fit it.

Index